*- Dr. Mitch Glaser, President, Chosen People Ministries International*

What a joy it is to know the Lord, who forgives our sins and grants the free gift of everlasting life. He gives to us His Holy Spirit, Who leads us into a deeper understanding of the Bible. God did not leave us without a guidebook!...This book makes a great devotional tool and discipleship "manual" for new believers or those who are getting serious about studying the Old Testament scriptures.

*- Larry Feldman, Messianic Congregation Planter and Leader of Shuvah Yisrael*

Harry has done an enjoyable and inspired work on the early chapters of the Book of Isaiah, presenting a refreshing, conservative, accurate view of the prophet Isaiah's message about the Messiah and the Messianic Age to come. Harry's Bible knowledge and clear theological thinking comes through his entire commentary. He deals well with the theological problems that come up in the text and also explains well the messianic passages that speak of *Yeshua* (Jesus) as the coming Messiah. He uses personal stories and illustrations to make the Scriptures come alive and apply to our everyday lives. I highly recommend reading this work.

*-Debbie Byars, former Controller at Ariel Ministries, and lover of the whole counsel of God thanks to Dr. Arnold Fruchtenbaum.*

I have been blessed to be a member of the same Messianic Congregation, *Shuvah Yisrael,* that Harry and Caty Mozell attend. The first thing you become aware of upon meeting Harry is that you are in the presence of a truly humble and godly man. Harry is a man of few words; however, when he speaks, I know that I want to listen and glean what I can from his wisdom and graciousness. In this book, Harry is bringing the reader to a neglected area of the Bible in our day, the *Tanakh* (Old Covenant.)

Isaiah can be a daunting book for many. Harry has taken his personal experiences and combined them with the study of Isaiah, making it easy to understand and humorous and, in so doing, leaving the reader wanting more of the Word. In his introduction, Harry writes, "In fact, you cannot understand the New unless you understand the Old, and the Old Testament writings are fulfilled in the New." This is true and sadly isn't widely taught today. You can't have a true understanding and knowledge of who God is without studying the *Tanakh*. Jeremiah 9:23-24 states that God is pleased when we understand and know Him, and in that He delights. Studying the Old Covenant is vital to our knowledge and understanding of the God of Abraham, Isaac, and Jacob, and the God of all who believe.

Harry so wants his Jewish brothers and sisters to know their Messiah. He brings this out in many places. I especially liked his words on Isaiah 1:16-18 on what God desires for His people. It is a great reminder that all things should be leading us to the Lord God and not to things that are unimportant. Harry is trying to lead people to look to the LORD alone. Regarding Isaiah 5:18-21, Harry writes, "We need to realize that we are not the center of the universe. We need to realize that the source of truth is greater than we are and outside of ourselves."

The Book of Isaiah is wonderful and filled with the wonder and holiness of the LORD. Harry has given us a way to make it a little more personal. *Enjoy!*

# REASONING TOGETHER

A Personal Account of
Isaiah Chapters 1 - 12

Harold Mozell

*Reasoning Together: A Personal Account of Isaiah Chapters 1 - 12*
© 2023 by Harold Mozell, www.facebook.com/harry.mozell.7, harmozell@gmail.com
Published by www.JHousePublishing.com under the *Purple Raiment* label, Keller, TX
www.jhousepublishing.com

ISBN: 978-1-950734-09-2
REL006120    RELIGION / Biblical Meditations / Old Testament
REL101000    MESSIANIC JUDAISM
BIO037000    BIOGRAPHY & AUTOBIOGRAPHY / Jewish

Unless otherwise noted, the Bible translation quoted in this book is the New American Standard Bible (NASB).

Holy Bible: New American Standard Bible – NASB 1977 Kindle Edition (Includes Translators' Notes), Copyright © 1960, 1962, 1963, 1968, 1971, 1972, 1973, 1975, 1977. Used by permission of the Lockman Foundation: A Corporation Not for Profit, La Habra, California. All Rights Reserved, www.lockman.org.

*American Standard Version,* public domain, original copyright 1901, accessed at Bible Gateway, www.biblegateway.com.

Darby Translation, public domain, first published in 1890 by John Nelson Darby.

Douay-Rheims 1899 American Edition, public domain.

ESV® Bible (The Holy Bible, English Standard Version®), copyright © 2001 by Crossway, a publishing ministry of Good News Publishers. Used by permission. All rights reserved. The ESV text may not be quoted in any publication made available to the public by a Creative Commons license. The ESV may not be translated into any other language.

King James Version of the Bible. Public Domain.

*La Santa Biblia, Nueva Versión Internacional®* NVI ® ©1999 *por la International Bible Society, Reservados todos los derechos en todo el mundo.*

New International Version®, NIV®. Copyright © 1973, 1978, 1984, 2011 by Biblica, Inc.™ Used by permission of Zondervan. All rights reserved worldwide. www.zondervan.com. The "NIV" and "New International Version" are trademarks registered in the United States Patent and Trademark Office by Biblica, Inc.™

*Tanakh:* The Holy Scriptures. PA: Jewish Publication Society. Public domain, 1917.

*Tanakh:* The JPS Bible, Pocket Edition (military) (English-only Tanakh). Lincoln, NE: University of Nebraska Press, 2008. Public domain.

Scripture quotations marked (TLB) are taken from *The Living Bible,* copyright © 1971 by Tyndale House Foundation. Used by permission of Tyndale House Publishers, Carol Stream, Illinois 60188. All rights reserved.

The Twenty-Four Books of the Holy Scriptures According to the Masoretic Text. English version translated and revised by Alexander Harkavy, ed. New York: The Hebrew Publishing Company, 1916. Public domain.

All rights reserved. No part of this publication may be reproduced or transmitted in any form or by any means without written permission of the publisher.

Editor: Joni Prinjinski
Paperback: Acid-free paper
Printed in the USA

Purple
Raiment

# Dedication

This book is dedicated to my father, **Norman Mozell,** who loved to write and, to my surprise, has passed this gift on to me. I know he would have been very proud to see this completed work.

# In Memoriam

## Zell Brooks

My beloved counselor and friend who instilled in me the powerful truth that our Lord has come to give life and to give it more abundantly.

## Bonnie White

Bonnie was always the shining light in our lives.

# Acknowledgements

I want to thank my loving wife Caty who has always been by my side and has faithfully walked with me through this adventure. I want to thank Bill and Bonnie White, our solid rocks through good times and hard times. I want to thank Joni Prinjinski who has always seen the potential of writing this book. I also want to thank Jean Kasdan, Sharon Pritzos, and Tracy Buck who, each in their own way, did a tremendous job proofreading this work.

# Table of Contents

Acknowledgements .................................................................................. xi
Foreword by Mitch Glaser ...................................................................... xv
Why I Wrote This Book ............................................................................ 1
Isaiah Chapter 1   A Call for Sincerity ....................................................... 5
Isaiah Chapter 2   A Call for a Humble Heart ......................................... 15
Isaiah Chapter 3   Judah's Collapse ......................................................... 25
Isaiah Chapter 4   A Sudden Transformation ......................................... 31
Isaiah Chapter 5   The Song of My Beloved Concerning His
  Vineyard ............................................................................................... 37
Isaiah Chapter 6   "Whom Shall I Send?" ............................................... 53
Isaiah Chapter 7   "Ask for a Sign" ......................................................... 67
Isaiah Chapter 8   Do Not Fear What They Fear .................................... 77
Isaiah Chapter 9   "And His Name Will Be Called" ............................... 85
Isaiah Chapter 10  Assyria's Conquests and Assyria's Demise ............ 121
Isaiah Chapter 11  Tremendous Hope for the Future ........................... 141
Isaiah Chapter 12  What to Say on that Day ........................................ 165
Isaiah Final Thoughts ............................................................................ 175
Update on Current Events .................................................................... 177
Appendix ............................................................................................... 179
Reference List ....................................................................................... 185
Study Outline ........................................................................................ 189
About the Author .................................................................................. 193

# Foreword by Mitch Glaser

## President, Chosen People Ministries International

How exciting it has been for me to write a recommendation for this delightful new book by my friend Harry Mozell on the topic of Isaiah, Chapters 1–12. I am so glad I was asked to write something about the book as I consider it a privilege to encourage Harry and get good Old Testament studies into the hands of believers.

Harry has been such an important part of my own life and journey in the faith. We met in New Jersey in the early 1970s. I was in Bible college and started a ministry on the Fairleigh Dickinson University campus. Harry was the first Jewish believer I met there, and we started a Bible study together. I remember quite well that we studied the book of James each and every week. Quite a few people began coming to the study, and it was a great joy and opportunity for both of us to become more familiar with the Word of God and to be discipled.

I love the intelligent simplicity of Harry's writing. He is true to the text which I deeply appreciate. I know the commentators that Harry used to develop his study, as we were both fellow Talbot Seminary students and flowed in the same theological streams. He used these writings wisely and judiciously. The book did not drag for one moment as it is written in a conversational and heartfelt style so that the reader does not get overwhelmed by Hebrew terms or theological issues but rather comes face to face with the underlying principles Isaiah was fond of communicating to his people.

I believe the book is well edited and will be very useful for personal Bible and group Bible studies. I hope that you will take the time to read it as I know you will enjoy the ways in which Harry helps you understand the message of the prophet in the first twelve critical chapters of the book.

For many years, Harry and I often sang together a popular messianic song entitled *Behold God Is My Salvation* as we toured together with the musical group, *Messiah's Shofar*. The song is based on the text found in Isaiah 12:2 - *"Behold, God is my salvation, I will trust and not be afraid; For the LORD GOD is my strength and song, And He has become my salvation."* What a joy it is to know the Lord, who forgives our sins and grants the free gift of everlasting life. He gives to us His Holy Spirit, Who leads us into a deeper understanding of the Bible. God did not leave us without a guidebook!

I am so grateful to Harry for sharing his personal experiences with the Lord which gives such "life" to the words of Isaiah. Thank you, Harry, for a wonderful effort. Your clear and thoughtful exposition enables us to better understand the holy and inspired words of the prophet Isaiah. This book makes a great devotional tool and discipleship "manual" for new believers or those who are getting serious about studying the Old Testament scriptures.

# Why I Wrote This Book

I decided to write this personal account of Isaiah Chapters 1 through 12 because I became aware that my Jewish family and friends and also my Christian friends did not really understand what I believe, or why.

I have found myself trapped in the middle of two worlds. Being Jewish and proclaiming *Yeshua*, Jesus, to be the Messiah immediately puts me at odds with the Jewish community, and understandably so. For centuries, the Jewish community has faced tremendous persecution from Christians in the name of Jesus. If you find this surprising, you might want to read the history of the Crusades and the Spanish Inquisition to see what I mean. Of course Jesus was also Jewish. His Hebrew name was *Yeshua*, meaning "God saves." His mother was *Miriam* (Mary) and His father was named *Yosef* (Joseph), good Hebrew names.

Logically, Jesus also would have been persecuted by the Church because of His Jewishness. In other words, Jesus would not have sanctioned and orchestrated persecutions toward His own people. He would have wanted the Church to emulate His compassion for the Jewish people. Of course there were sincere Christians in the midst of this quagmire who did not follow the biases of the organized Church but were instead amiable to the Jewish people.

So on one hand, being Jewish and believing in Jesus has created tension for me with my Jewish friends and family. On the other hand, being Jewish and believing in Jesus has also put me at odds with the Christian community because of bias against Jewish culture. That is, if I insist on maintaining my Jewish culture and identity, I often experience a big disconnect. My Christian friends have a hard time understanding why I prefer to celebrate Hanukkah and Passover over Christmas and Easter. They assume that when you receive Messiah into your heart and life, you will give up your Jewish culture and heritage and instead adopt a cultural Christian heritage. However, from my perspective, I have found the Jewish roots of my faith to be deeply meaningful and enriching.

So I have written this work as an attempt to reach out to my family and Jewish friends along with my Christian friends.

Isaiah Chapters 1 – 12 is a unique passage because not only does it provide a clear picture of God's desire for Israel to come to Him, but also provides thought-provoking reasons to believe in or trust in the Messiah through the prophet Isaiah's vision of who the Messiah will be. Intertwined in this work I have included my life's experiences in the hope that they will encourage and enlighten the hearts of those who are willing to consider these questions for themselves. This book, in a sense, is autobiographical.

Keep in mind that these first twelve chapters of Isaiah can be intense and at the same time emotionally deep and meaningful. As you read, you will find many issues to ponder and wrestle with, as I have. Approach this study from the perspective of one who has been on a spiritual journey.

As we enter into this first chapter of Isaiah, I need to let you know that I am not entering into it blindly but am using a few sources to help me along the way. I am mainly referring to Leupold's *Exposition of Isaiah,* Ironside's *The Prophet Isaiah,* Keil and Delitzsch's *Commentary on the Old Testament,* and a tape series and Bible Commentary on Isaiah by Arnold Fruchtenbaum, published by Ariel Ministries. I also have a few ideas of my own which I sheepishly contribute because Scripture warns believers: *Let not many of you become teachers, my brethren, knowing that as such we will incur a stricter judgment* (James 3:1). The Bible version I am using is the New American Standard Bible (NASB) (1977), and I do refer to other translations and Hebrew and Spanish texts when I can.

I reference the New Testament at times in this work. If you would, the Hebrew term for the New Testament would be the *Brit Chadashah*, "The Covenant – New." You may ask, "Why? Isn't that a Christian book?" In response I would say that the New Testament is a very Jewish book. All the writers of the New Testament were Jewish except for Luke, who was a doctor, and that's close enough to being Jewish. The concepts taught in the *Brit Chadashah* reflect and mirror the concepts taught in the *Tanakh*, the Old Testament. In fact, you cannot understand the New unless you understand the Old, and the Old Testament writings are fulfilled in the New.

You may have noticed that I have dated many sections throughout the study. Originally, I was emailing this study out weekly to interested readers. The dates that are placed before portions of the readings represent the time I had originally sent out the emails. I wanted you to have a sense of my journey through time as I wrote this work.

As things go, the time between posts became longer and longer, and I eventually stopped sending out the study, but I kept writing. By the end of Chapter 10, I started documenting current events before continuing with the study for each section.

In order to fully grasp the sense of this study, please take time and read each chapter of Isaiah prior to reading the study for that chapter. I've even included little reminders when we are about to start a new chapter.

Although it took me 14 years to put together all the studies, I promise you it will not take 14 years to go through it all!

# Isaiah Chapter 1    A Call for Sincerity

2/10/07

"I have just read Chapter 1." ___ yes

### Isaiah's Introduction to His Book of Prophecy (Isaiah 1:1)

Isaiah starts with an introduction giving a history of his ministry through four kings of Judah: Uzziah, Jotham, Ahaz, and Hezekiah. You might compare him to the Queen of England, who held her position even though various Prime Ministers came to office and then moved on. Only in Isaiah's case, the kings of Judah did not move on but basically died!

You might be wondering why Isaiah says "four kings of *Judah*" instead of four kings of *Israel*. Well, here's a little background. By the time Isaiah wrote this prophecy, the nation of Israel that had once been one kingdom was now divided into two kingdoms, a northern and a southern one. The northern kingdom was called Israel and was made up of ten tribes. The southern kingdom was called Judah and was made up of two tribes. Isaiah's prophecies warn both kingdoms of destruction ahead! While judgment is ahead, Isaiah also relays God's promise to eventually restore.

When David was King, around 1000 BCE (Before the Christian Era), he was the king over all twelve tribes of Israel, each one named after one of the twelve sons of Jacob. David's son Solomon kept the kingdom intact and increased the kingdom's prominence. Because of Solomon, Israel as a nation was known far and wide for all its glory.

How did Israel become split in two? Solomon's son Rehoboam, to his demise, did not listen to the wise counsel of his elders but listened to the advice of his young contemporaries instead. A political divide resulted in which the ten northern tribes split off under the leadership of a man named Jeroboam and created their own kingdom, the Kingdom of Israel. The two remaining southern tribes, Judah and Benjamin, became the Kingdom of Judah.

As God warned Isaiah in his vision, Israel's conduct was so gross that His judgment was already on the way. The mighty Assyrians were now coming down to conquer the Kingdom of Israel.

Isaiah wrote during this Assyrian Captivity, in the late 800s and early 700s BCE. Isaiah also wrote of Judah's future demise via the coming Babylonian Captivity, which happened 200 years later.

It is the timing of Isaiah's vision and prophecy that makes his foretelling so profound because he describes the coming of Messiah in great detail, as if someone else wrote it after the fact. Keep in mind that Isaiah writes with a sense of God's compassion and love for His people, and yet he communicates a great sense of God's holiness (Fruchtenbaum, cassette 1, side one).

Reminder: In order to fully grasp the sense of the study, please take time and read each chapter of Isaiah prior to reading the study for that chapter.

### *The Courtroom (Isaiah 1:2-15)*

As we pick up our study today, remember that Isaiah starts his written book of prophecy with an introduction giving a history of his ministry through four kings of Judah: Uzziah, Jotham, Ahaz, and

Hezekiah. Then Isaiah immediately makes a declaration similar to a judge about to preside over his courtroom:

*Listen, O heavens, and hear, O earth; for the LORD speaks* (1:2a).

According to Bible scholar Arnold Fruchtenbaum (cassette 1, side one), this statement is what the Eternal Judge would say to the courtroom, just as we would hear today, "Hear ye, hear ye! This court is now in session."

Isaiah's announcement of verse 2 is the verdict placed upon the defendant, Israel. The commentators refer to it as an "indictment." Of course, before the verdict, the Judge has a few comments to make (continuing in verse 2). *"Sons I have reared and brought up, but they have revolted against Me."* Then in verse 3, Isaiah continues with the same theme: *"An ox knows its owner, and a donkey its master's manger, but Israel does not know, My people do not understand."*

I have never had children, but I have watched others struggle with their siblings not listening, going off on their own way, thinking they know it all. I've watched parents express their pain as their kids make wrong choices, knowing the consequences that lie ahead for them. The Lord is communicating here that He understands how this feels, and maybe we can understand how He feels when we make dumb choices.

Even the ox and the donkey know their masters! The ox and donkey are not known for their intellectual prowess, and even they know better. As Fruchtenbaum notes in his cassette series on Isaiah, today we have the same expressions, referring to the "dumb ox" or the "stupid ass," and yet these animals have more sense than Israel has at times to do what's right (cassette 1, side one).

Verse 4 starts with an *"oy!"* Actually the Hebrew word is *"hoy."* You will see it in various English translations as "alas," "ah," and "woe." *Alas, sinful nation.* Isaiah here is writing to the northern kingdom Israel, but the principles of his exhortation carry over to the southern kingdom of Judah as well, because Judah was following along the same path.

Also in verse 4 you see the term *the Holy One of Israel.* This phrase will continue throughout Isaiah's prophesy: *They have despised the Holy One of Israel.* The contrast here is astounding! Israel's actions and attitude are placed against the standard of Holy God.

Verses 5b and 6a continue with this theme of the horrifying decline of God's people. *The whole head is sick, and the whole heart is faint. From the sole of the foot even to the head there is nothing sound in it.* It would be wiser to ask that the *Ruach Ha Khodesh*, the Holy Spirit, fill us from head to toe.

Verses 7 through 10 describe the consequences of Israel's attitude: her cities burned, fields devoured, and her land overthrown by strangers. Yet there is an element of hope, too. The Lord always preserves a "remnant," a group comprised of those who still believe. This theme of the faithful remnant carries throughout the Scriptures as well.

We read in verses 11-15 that our Lord was specifically concerned with the form of worship at that time, doing the right things, but with formalism and not with heart, offering prayers out of obligation to the Lord, but not because of wanting to commune with Him or know Him. And the worst thing about it was thinking it was okay.

### What God Desires for His People (Isaiah 1:16-18)

As we continue on to verses 16 and 17 in Isaiah Chapter 1, we see what the resolution is in God's eyes. What is right to do is to *"wash yourselves, make yourselves clean; remove the evil of your deeds from My sight. Cease to do evil, learn to do good; seek justice, reprove the ruthless, defend the orphan, plead for the widow."* That's all nice and good, literally; but we can't do all this in our own strength, and we will get into that next time. Until then, pray, ask the Lord for wisdom and insight, read through Chapter 1 again, and even read ahead. It can only be a benefit for us.

I have been in enough counseling sessions through the years to realize that people can change. Many folks who do not know our Lord can achieve personal changes that can result in happy and productive lives. They can stop drinking and doing drugs. They can save their marriages, spend more time with their kids, be faithful in their jobs, and be honest with their money. That's why we have so many "self help" books on the market today.

Yet God is looking for a kind of change that only He can produce. And it doesn't involve simply being moral. It's a change of our very nature. Yes, mankind can "turn over a new leaf" so to speak. However, the problem God is addressing here is not the living of a good life, but the admission of our weakness and need. The Jewish people mentioned in Isaiah 1 were doing everything right, to the letter. They were executing the sacrificial system required for remission of sins perfectly. They were praying the right prayers and saying the correct words. What more could God want?

Well, the Lord wanted Israel to stop looking at Israel and start looking at God. How many times have we been in a church or synagogue and heard the people raving about the great worship team, dance team, or the beautiful Hebrew singing, or even the well-constructed and thorough Bible study presented that day? Or perhaps we admired the beautiful choir, the massive pipe organ, or the magnificent stained glass windows. Maybe we boasted about how our ministry team can pray for people and watch them get healed and how special and holy we must be. We may meditate on how we keep the Sabbath, light the candles, don't shop on Saturdays, and keep *kosher*, and pat ourselves on the back for how faithful we are. We may feel that the "other" group, sadly, is missing out on God's blessings.

Well, it's not that God doesn't like a good choir, or beautiful artwork, or appreciate that someone is willing to set one day aside for spiritual rest, but He wants communion with us, too. Look at verse 18:

> *"Come now, and let us reason together,"*
> *Says the LORD.*
> *"Though your sins are as scarlet,*
> *They will be as white as snow;*
> *Though they are red like crimson,*
> *They will be like wool."*

Israel's sins were very dark at that time. They were flirting with idol worship, making alliances with evil nations, and yet paying homage to God, at least outwardly. Don't get the wrong idea. There were some sincere believers present as well, for God always preserves a remnant who is faithful to Him; but the political scene was not good. Kind of like today ….

So God is willing to "reason" with Israel. He is offering to come to terms. By His power He is offering to change the color of their sins from ones that are a kind of dark red that attracts attention and is reminiscent of blood guiltiness, and change them to a pure white as of snow or wool. That's fascinating. We'll talk more about that next time!

## Color Systems in Language (Isaiah 1:18b-31)

Did you know that different languages have varied color systems? Some languages have only five colors, and some have hundreds! In languages with basic color systems, the colors are distinguished by how bright or dull they are or how cool or warm they are. Also some languages use the grayscale which is a mix of black, white, and gray. The cool colors would be blues and greens, and the warm colors would be yellows and reds. I was talking to our maintenance man in my apartment complex, and he was telling me that some apartment interior walls are painted with "Navajo white" and some with "Swiss coffee." Well, that's English for you. One of my adult Vietnamese students in ESL (English as a Second Language) class described what we would call a blue/green as "Yamaha." The reason is that Yamaha makes a popular motorcycle that features that color. Hebrew has a limited color scheme and has to describe many colors by identifying them with known objects. For example, the Hebrew word *edom* refers to a red soil or red clay color. Hebrew does not have a separate color for green and yellow, but lumps them together as an agricultural or natural color.

## God's Transforming Color Scheme

In Isaiah 1:18b we see examples of color comparisons in Hebrew. *"Though your sins are as scarlet, they will be as white as snow; though they are red like crimson, they will be like wool."* The descriptions of these red colors are actually a dark kind of red. The crimson listed in the second sentence can be a kind of purple. Even in Spanish, this idea holds true as the second phrase reads, *"¿Son rojos como la pu'rpura? ¡Quedar'an como la lana!"* (New International Version – Spanish translation).

The commentators point out that the red of 1:18 is symbolic of the blood-guiltiness of Israel's sin, and stands out among other colors. It would be a mistake, though, to equate the red of blood-guiltiness with the Lamb's blood, shed on the altar or Messiah's blood shed for us. Messiah's blood was the kind of blood that gives life; and when He shed it, He poured out His life for us. Makes sense. In our bloodstream is all we need to live: oxygen, nutrients, vitamins, minerals, disease fighters, platelets, etc. The blood is the sustenance of life for us.

But blood-guiltiness is something different. It means we have literally or symbolically taken another's life, and we are guilty. The Lord has offered Israel a way to change the state of the nation from one of representing the red of blood-guiltiness to a state of being white as snow or wool! How can that happen? Obviously it couldn't be accomplished by Israel's actions or deeds because that method was not working. They were keeping the sacrificial system to the letter. This change from red to white could only occur through the enabling power of God, Himself, and ultimately through His shedding of life-giving blood. All Israel had to do was to *"consent and obey"* as mentioned in verse 19. God wanted His people to turn to Him in attitude. If Israel instead chose to *"refuse and rebel,"* as God says in verse 20, His judgment could be the only result.

In the *Brit Chadashah,* meaning "Covenant – New," referring to The New Testament, we can see God's unique, revolutionary plan to free us from sin.

> *⁸ For by grace you have been saved through faith; and that not of yourselves, it is the gift of God; ⁹ not as a*

*result of works, so that no one may boast.* ¹⁰ *For we are **His workmanship**, created in Messiah Yeshua for good works, which God prepared beforehand so that we would walk in them.* (Ephesians 2:8-10) [The bold emphasis is mine.]

Sadly, Israel chose the path of thinking they could do it on their own. Chapters 2 and 3 of Isaiah, as well as verses 19 through 30 of Chapter 1, talk of the good and the bad ahead, the blessings of the Millennial Kingdom to come, contrasted with the impending judgments now coming, from the captivities by Assyria and Babylon, and culminating in the future Tribulation period.

# Isaiah Chapter 2  A Call for a Humble Heart

3/5/2007

"I have just read Chapter 2." ___ yes

### Isaiah Shares a Refreshing Second Vision, One of Hope (Isaiah 2:1, 2)

As we leave Isaiah Chapter 1 and venture into Chapters 2 to 4 it is important to note that God is a Father. His concern is for the fatherless and the widow. Looking back to Chapter 1, we see that verse 17b reads, *"Defend the orphan, plead for the widow."* God's concern is also found in verse 1:23b: *They do not defend the orphan, nor does the widow's plea come before them.* You will see this theme not only in Isaiah but throughout the Scriptures.

Chapter two starts with a one-verse introduction: *The word which Isaiah the son of Amoz saw concerning Judah and Jerusalem.* In Chapter 1, as Fruchtenbaum (cassette 1, side one) explains, we can also see this pattern as it starts with the similar phrase: *The vision of Isaiah the son of Amoz, concerning Judah and Jerusalem which he saw ....* So it is safe to conclude that the *vision* of Chapter 1:1 is somehow the same as the *word* of Chapter 2:1; and the question arises, "How can one see a word?" Was it something that was impressed upon Isaiah's spirit, something he received or perceived, or was it something he literally read as in a vision? We cannot know, but it is wonderful to note that God can communicate in mysterious ways, and we are not in a real place to analyze or understand it.

The message was concerning Judah, but *especially* Jerusalem. Apparently the citizens of Jerusalem believed that they were privileged to live in a special city, and that God would defend her no matter what. What harm could come to God's city? Did we not have the same attitude here in the U.S. before 9/11? How humbling it was for us all when New York proved to be vulnerable. What we took for granted as our secure homeland was seemingly and abruptly slipping out of our hands.

As a means of encouragement, God shows us the hope of a glorious future for Judah and Jerusalem *in the last days* (2:2). He reveals this hope before He presents for us the coming conditions of the Tribulation period (Fruchtenbaum, cassette 1, side two). You might be wondering what the Tribulation period is. It's a terrible period on earth in the future just before the time of the Messiah's return. It's a time when we will be following a false messiah in the hope that he will bring peace to the earth. He will unite the world economically, politically, and spiritually but will be, from the core, evil. As a result, the Lord will bring judgment upon the earth.

One of the best illustrations of spiritual encouragement is found in *The Pilgrim's Progress*, the classic work by John Bunyan. Christian, the main character in the book, had been through many trials: facing Apollyon, struggling through the Slough of Despond, and enduring the mocking from the citizens of Vanity Fair. As a reprieve, he was led to the high lands, where shepherds ministered to him and encouraged him. From such a high vantage point, he was able to see where he had been and could see where he was going, to the Celestial City. In our walk with our Lord, we can look forward to these times of refreshment and feeding.

Next time we will look more closely at verses 1 through 3, and it is encouraging to note that a couple of Messianic song writers have made valuable contributions to our worship through these verses in Isaiah. Marc Chopinski from the group called *Israel's Hope* has written a song called *Come Let Us Go Up* (see verse 3), and Ted Pearce has written a work called *Come House of Jacob* (see verse 5). I'm sure you can Google these names and titles to find more info, if you would like, and maybe listen to these beautiful songs.

**Come Let Us Go Up (Isaiah 2:1-3)**

The passage in Isaiah 2:2-4 is almost identical to that found in Micah 4:1-3, below:

*[1] And it will come about in the last days*

*That the mountain of the house of the LORD*

*Will be established as the chief of the mountains.*

*It will be raised above the hills,*

*And the peoples will stream to it.*

*[2] And many nations will come and say,*

*"Come and let us go up to the mountain of the LORD*

*And to the house of the God of Jacob,*

*That He may teach us about His ways*

*And that we may walk in His paths."*

*For from Zion will go forth the law,*

*Even the word of the LORD from Jerusalem.*

*³ And He will judge between many peoples*

*And render decisions for mighty, distant nations.*

*Then they will hammer their swords into plowshares*

*And their spears into pruning hooks;*

*Nation will not lift up sword against nation,*

*And never again will they train for war.*

So who copied from whom since they prophesied in similar times? We can't say. Maybe they both were inspired by the same *Ruach*, or Spirit, or by an "anonymous earlier prophet" (Leupold, p. 74). I remember Chuck Smith, founder of Calvary Chapel and a mainstay of the Jesus Movement of the 1970s, saying that he would often listen to the various Christian speakers on the radio on a particular day to see what message the Holy Spirit was giving to the body of believers that day.

The passage talks of the latter or *last days*. This term can go deep into the future – or not as far into the future – depending on the prophet describing it. Isaiah uses the term as meaning "far into the Messianic Age," that is, referring to the Millennial Kingdom, and this time would lie beyond the point of the return of the Messiah (Leupold, p. 74).

Verse 2 talks of the establishment of *the mountain of the house of the LORD*. It will be *the chief of the mountains* of the LORD, and will be *raised above the hills; and all the nations will stream to it*. Well, what is this mountain? Some say it is the highest of all the mountains, the most prominent and glorious one. "Whether it had physical exultation that raised it higher than all other mountains, or whether it was surrounded by a glorious light, we are unable to determine" (Leupold, p.76). I think rather it is a small mountain such as Mount Zion, one that is small but mighty.

Isn't that the nature of God to be humble in regard to status? He did not want Israel to have a king, but rather wanted her to be ruled by Judges. He did not want a glorious building to house the tabernacle, but was content with placing it in tents. In contrast, isn't it the nature of man to want the biggest and best of all things? Mankind wants the largest house, the most luxurious car, the finest jewelry, and the latest fashion. I think God is content with the simple things.

The term *chief* of the mountains is in Hebrew *be rosh,* "at the head" (Leupold, p.76). We use the same term for *Rosh Ha Shana* or "head of the year." So this particular mountain is the governmental authority that is the head of other, smaller governmental entities. And all the nations will "stream" or "flow" to it.

Verse 3 continues, *And many peoples will come and say, "Come let us go up to the mountain of the LORD, to the house of the God of Jacob."* Here we have a play on words, because in Chapter 1, verse 1, God was inviting Israel to the table with the words, *"Come now, and let us reason together."* In these future times, the nations, themselves, and not God, will be giving the invitation. Wow, what a contrast to today, where the nations do not want to say that there is indeed a God, or if they do, to acknowledge that He is the God of the Jewish people, the God of Jacob.

More on that next time!

## More Encouragement, Eagerness, and Invitations (Isaiah 2:3-5)

Isaiah 2, verse 3, states:

> *And many peoples will come and say, "Come, let us go up to the mountain of the LORD, to the house of the God of Jacob; that He may teach us concerning His ways, and that we may walk in His paths." For the law will go forth from Zion, and the word of the LORD from Jerusalem.*

These people wanted to be taught. As Leupold stated, "Once there was arrogant pride; now humble inquiry" (p. 77). What attracted them was God's revealed truth.

Notice the comparison between *the law* and *the word*. Essentially they are one and the same. Sometimes we put too much emphasis on the concept of the law being something we need "to do," as compared to the law being something we need "to be," indicating our desire to emulate the moral character of God, the goodness, fairness, justice, and uprightness of God.

At this future time, the Lord will judge between the nations and will render decisions for many peoples. It will be the Lord acting as Judge, and not the World Court nor the United Nations (U.N.). Speaking of the United Nations, I remember my dad proudly remarking that their motto, written near the entrance of the facility, was a phrase taken from the Jewish Scriptures! It reads, "Let Us Beat Swords into Plowshares." Yet I don't think he knew it was taken from Isaiah Chapter 2, verse 4: *And they will hammer their swords into plowshares, and their spears into pruning hooks.* The verse continues, *Nation will not lift up sword against nation, and never again will they learn war.* The U.N. cannot bring about this peace because the problem is bigger than mankind can handle. Think about it; in this future time the weapons of war will no longer be of any use for us, nor the learning of the techniques of war (Leupold, p.78). No more need for nuclear, chemical, or biological warfare, and no more need for military academies and war rooms! And all this will be the benefit of submitting to the Word of the Lord.

Verse 5 begins with yet another "Come let us" invitation. *Come, house of Jacob, and let us walk in the light of the LORD.* It is a conclusion of the previous thought, and also a transition into the next section of the text. In a way, it is encouraging to see that God has let us know the glorious end before the beginning of the hard times. He is revealing the victorious reign of Messiah before His warning about the harshness of the Tribulation period yet to come. We will explore this further next time!

## To See or Not to See (Isaiah 2:6)

Sometimes I lose my glasses and then I find myself in a dilemma. I need my glasses to see where my glasses are. In the same way Israel needed the Lord's enabling strength to find Him, and if they did not seek the Lord, they would not have the ability to find Him and would stumble around in their own strength.

Isaiah 2 continues with this theme in mind. Israel had found substitutes for the true and living God, and she was not able to see clearly enough to recognize her mistake. Verse 6 implies that there were influences affecting Israel *from the east,* indicating the rising Assyrian presence, and from the "west," the soothsayers like the Philistines (Leupold, p. 79). A soothsayer is one who foretells or predicts the future as in a "fortune teller." In our society we think of fortune telling via psychics, palm readers, tarot card readers, etc., as a kind of fun thing to do and yet the Lord sees it as dealing with real darkness and consistently warns against its practice.

### *Silver and Gold Have I None (Isaiah 2:7-11)*

Verse 7 continues that Israel had placed great value in *silver and gold,* and also in the abundance of *horses* and *chariots.* We do the same. As a nation we value the power of our economy as our security, and we rest in our military might. Think of how we panic when the stock market drops a few hundred points. And we want to make sure we have the military upper hand over our adversaries: China, Russia, North Korea, Iran, and whoever else. Who would have guessed that the threat of "terrorism" would be our Achilles' heel?

Israel had also given prominence to her *idols* (verse 8). They were of great value, a family treasure, made of silver and gold. The poor had to make them of wood. But the word here for idol in Hebrew is *elil*, indicating that they were a "thing of naught, weak, feeble, worthless, insufficient." As Ironside asserts, they will prove to be "powerless to deliver those who put their trust in them" (p. 21).

Verses 9 through 11 magnify this theme and bring us forward to the time of reckoning in the last days. At that time, there will be no turning back.

The answer for us then is to take everything we have, all we've worked for, everything we value, and give them to our Lord. Do not let the security they provide be a substitute for the peace and security God provides. Do not depend on them. Depend on the Lord to provide for us all we need. Thank Him for His provision and rest in His love and security.

### A Day of Reckoning (Isaiah 2:12-22)

*For the LORD of hosts will have a day of reckoning* (verse 12). I remember in my fanatical days, when I was a youth of 19 or 20. I had just come to know the Lord and was a student at Fairleigh Dickinson University in New Jersey. I was writing articles in the school newspaper about the issue of *Yeshua* (Jesus) being the Jewish Messiah. We had a book table and weekly Bible studies. We would hand out literature and put up Jews for Jesus posters, which, by the way, were promptly taken down. And I was given the nicknames "Hallelujah Harry" and "Sodom and Gomorrah Mozell" by the newspaper editors. The reason was that I would look at the sky and see the tremendous and yet glorious storm clouds coming our way and would get on my knees and say, "Can't you see that He's coming?! Get yourselves ready!" A little extreme. Not a good way to make friends.

I can see why Isaiah was not popular in his day because he was a bearer of convicting and not so good news of Israel's future. There will be a day of reckoning. *Reckoning* is the act of counting or computing. It's like an itemized bill or statement of a sum due. And the reckoning is *against everyone who is proud and lofty, and against everyone who is lifted up* (see verse 12). It's better to be careful of our power. We may be in positions of responsibility and authority, and the temptation would be to say, "Hey, I must be hot stuff. I must be something in this world!" The temptation would be to look at those under us as not as important. Maybe they don't have a respectable job, or not enough money, or don't dress well, or live in a not-so-nice area. I'm telling you that God has a very different perspective. He looks at the motives of the heart and is not really concerned about our great status.

Verses 13 through 18 provide a list of all the things that were a source of pride for Israel and proved to be false hopes and false security for Israel.

In that time *men will go into caves of the rocks, and into the holes of the ground* (verse 19). The caves were a place of hiding and refuge. David hid from Saul in caves. Shepherds would use caves to house their sheep and to protect them from wolves. As a side note, if you like the works of Leon Uris, you will find that in his novel *The Haj,* Haj Ibraham took his family to the caves of Qumran to hide from Muslim radicals. The symbolism is strikingly apparent. The people at the time of God's judgment will be running from the *terror of the LORD, and before the splendor of His majesty* (verse 19).

Isaiah tells us in verses 20-22 that when they were running to the caves for refuge they were also taking their idols with them! Were they their most valued possessions? The idols, or "nothings" as the Hebrew suggests, proved to be of no value; and they cast them *to the moles and the bats* (verse 20). "Moles and bats inhabit dark and repulsive places," commented Leupold (p. 84). Fruchtenbaum adds "moles and bats are semi-blind creatures. So the people worshipped the very thing that could not see and could not help them" (p. 51). Verses 21 and 22 again refer to the last days when the realization exists that there will be no place to hide.

When we see a magnificent storm approaching, we can see the power and might and glory of the storm and yet fear the destruction it could bring. In contrast, when we are in the Lord, we will rest in His glory and power and majesty.

# Isaiah Chapter 3   Judah's Collapse

3/28/2007

"I have just read Chapter 3." ___ yes

**Losses and Role Reversals (Isaiah 3:1-8)**

Isaiah Chapter 3 opens with the repeated phrase *Jerusalem and Judah* (verse 1):

*For behold, the Lord GOD of hosts is going to remove from*
   *Jerusalem and Judah*
*Both supply and support, the whole supply of bread,*
*And the whole supply of water;*

The term *supply and support* is a play on words like the expression *bag and baggage* (Leupold, p. 89).

Bread and water are our basic needs. Those of us who live in Southern California have a taste of this idea of supply and support because we are totally dependent on water from the Colorado River and the San Francisco Bay, and it is supplied to us through major engineering projects. I was at a conference for teachers of English as a Second Language (ESL) this past weekend in San Diego, and a group of us instructors were taking a taxi back to the train station in order to return to Los Angeles. During the ride, the subject of possible rain came up. One of us stated, "Boy, we really need rain." The taxi driver perked up and replied, "We don't need rain." We replied, "What!? Why do you say that?" The taxi driver simply responded, "We have all the sprinklers to water everything around here." I suppose that's one way of looking at it.

As we continue through the list of losses that threatened Judah, also taken away will be *the mighty man and the warrior, the judge and the prophet, the diviner and the elder* (verse 3:2). Notice that the *diviner* is just as important as the others. Unfortunately, occultism played a prominent role in the life of the nation. Such is mentioned again as the list continues in verse 3, *The captain of fifty and the honorable man, the counselor and the expert artisan, and the **skillful enchanter*** [bold used for emphasis].

Why was there no mention of a "king"? Leupold suggests that possibly it is because of the king's total ineffectiveness (p. 90). At that time, the citizens will be looking for anyone to rule over them, even *mere lads* and *capricious children* (verse 4), so that the inexperienced and irresponsible would be raised to positions of authority (p. 90).

Verse 5 continues that the traditions of the old and venerable will no longer be respected. Leupold put it this way, "Young fellows following ... the merest whim of the moment throw such sound traditions to the winds" (p. 90). I'm reminded of the phrase, "Teach your parents well" from a song by Crosby, Stills and Nash entitled "Teach your Children." Maybe some of you younger readers have heard of this 70s group? Well, as a society, we were going through many value changes at that time, and the thought of teaching one's parents was something completely new. The song lyrics imply that the children needed to teach the parents because the parents were not able to be examples for their children. The concept of a parent's life experiences passed on to the next generation was compromised.

Verses 6 through 8 continue this thought by the mere fact that those who are assumed to be in leadership refused to take on that responsibility. So the lesson for us to receive is, don't be afraid to take responsibility.

We will explore Judah's predicament further next time, but I need to warn you that some gender issues will be coming up, and it may prove controversial.

## One's Heart Brings Consequences, Good or Bad (Isaiah 3:9-15)

Isaiah Chapter 3, verse 9, says, *The expression of their faces bears witness against them. And they display their sin like Sodom; they do not even conceal it.* In this case, their facial expressions were displayed unashamedly. It's an advanced state of sinfulness, out in the open, not done in secret or concealed. How opposite this is to the experience of Moses, not being able to look at the glory of the Lord's face, and the people of Israel not able to look at Moses' face when he descended from the mountain. Even in Isaiah 6, Isaiah could not look at the holiness of the Lord, but fell down before the Lord and said he was a man of unclean lips.

Verses 10 and 11 are similar to Psalm 1 and Jeremiah 17:5-8, where the direction of a man's heart will bring about blessings or cursings.

Verse 12 continues, *Oh My people! Their oppressors are children, and women rule over them. Oh My people! Those who guide you lead you astray, and confuse the direction of your paths.* Women were put in a negative light when placed together with children in their ability to lead. Uh-Oh. What did I do? I said the politically unmentionable. Well, many women proved to be great leaders in the

Scriptures. Deborah was a powerful Judge, and Queen Esther rescued the Jewish population in Shushan. In the *Brit Chadashah*, the New Testament, Priscilla worked with her husband Aquila in a powerful ministry, and Philip had four daughters who were notable for their gifts in prophecy. In modern times we can look at Golda Meir and Margaret Thatcher as effective leaders. Am I forgiven now?

Verse 13 reminds us that God will stand up for justice. Verse 14 declares, *The LORD enters into judgment with the elders and princes of His people, "It is you who have devoured the vineyard; the plunder of the poor is in your houses."* You will see in Chapter 5 how the Lord compares the people of Israel to His vineyard. The image of taking items of value from the poor and displaying them in their homes is striking. Verse 15 describes one who is forced to lie face down only to have his face pushed into the sand. *"What do you mean by crushing My people and grinding the face of the poor?" declares the Lord GOD of hosts.*

### *Figurehead or True Leader? (Isaiah 3:12-15; Isaiah 4:1)*

4/8/2007

Let's take another look at the poor leadership going on in Judah, and the consequences that follow. Verse 12 of Isaiah 3 is referring to men as leaders who are not strong leaders and are acting as inexperienced children or "girly men" as one of our California governors once put it. At times, in the absence of healthy masculine leadership, tyrannical women have taken over as did Jezebel and Athaliah in 1 Kings 18 and 2 Kings 11. In this case, those whose business it was to guide the nation were the ones that misled it.

Verses 13 and 14 remind us of the trial setting of Chapter 1, verse 2. The Lord *stands to judge the people.* The judgment is that they *"have devoured the vineyard."* The ones who were given the responsibility to cultivate and protect the vineyard, or symbolically, Israel, were the very ones who devastated it. The leaders were supposed to be the protectors of the helpless (verse 15). Leupold described it as "the height of criminal action" (p. 94).

### Outer or Inner Beauty (Isaiah 3:16-26)
4/8/2007

Verse 16 introduces the indictment of the vain and frivolous (Leupold, p. 96). The term *daughters of Zion* was an honored description. Daughters of Zion were ones who had, as Leupold states (p. 96), "a noble destiny," because "women can exercise a tremendous influence for good or bad on the nation." In contrast, here the term is used in a negative sense because their behavior was proud and self-centered. Look at these descriptions. They walked with *heads held high* and had *seductive eyes,* attracting attention to themselves. They walked with *mincing steps. Mincing* is an adjective meaning "affectedly refined or dainty." "They promoted their charm as mere objects of beauty" (p. 96). They were "divas," if you will. What happened to inner integrity and inner beauty?

Now there's good in wanting to be attractive; it's normal and healthy, but what matters here is our focus. We can focus on glorifying the Lord in how He made each of us, instead of glorying in how stylish or beautiful one is, or how this woman looks better and has "spent more money" than that woman on a particular day.

Verses 18-24 give us a long list of articles women were donning. Obviously not all women were wearing all that was listed here at the same time. It's the astounding number of items worn that should impress us. Also, the amount of money invested in what is described as vain and frivolous beauty is a consideration. Please note: Not all women in the society were this way. The Lord always has left Himself a remnant of women with integrity, women who knew where their inner beauty came from. Sadly, the women of Israel in Isaiah's day were to experience the other side, *branding instead of beauty*, and were to become repulsive to be seen. They were to be led away as captives who have been humbled; *instead of sweet perfume there will be putrefaction; instead of a belt, a rope* (verse 24).

You may be asking, "Why is Isaiah being so hard on the women of his day?" Keep in mind that men have issues too! Generally, men want to be heroes, to be providers, to be strong, and to be noble. A lot of men will become "macho men" in order to prove they have these qualities, but inwardly they know they lack. They put on a show for others. How offensive and insulting it must have seemed for the leaders of Isaiah's day to hear over and over again, from passage to passage, that they were actually brutally inadequate in their positions of authority.

Because the Hebrew text does not have chapter and verse, Chapter 3 actually ends with the statement in Chapter 4, verse 1. Isaiah concludes this section with the grim reality that women, who normally were the ones to be pursued, were reduced to pursuing men, any man who would take away their reproach and give them a married name. Will this happen to our society? Are the values promoted on TV, the media, magazines, and the web promoting self and outward beauty? Where is the value of others and the value of inner beauty being promoted?

# Isaiah Chapter 4   A Sudden Transformation

5/12/07

"I have just read Chapter 4." ___ yes

As mentioned in the last section, verse 1 of Chapter 4 actually fits as the last verse of Chapter 3. So let's continue in verse 2 of Chapter 4.

### The Branch Introduced (Isaiah 4:2)

The passage we're starting with today covers verses 2 to 6 since verse 1 was the conclusion of Chapter 3. It is an abrupt transition or change from verse 1 to verse 2, and there is no indication as to why Isaiah wrote it this way or why there was a change of attitude on the part of God. He is merciful.

Verse 2 reads, *In that day the Branch of the LORD will be beautiful and glorious, and the fruit of the earth will be the pride and the adornment of the survivors of Israel.* So we read, *In that day.* What day? There are differing views on what constitutes the "Day of the Lord." According to Leupold, it is not only a day of judgment, but also a day when "great things are achieved. It's when the time has come for God to act" (p. 102).

It is in this passage that Isaiah introduces the idea of *the Branch of the LORD*. Apparently the Hebrew word *tsemach* cannot be translated fully in English. It's not really a branch or a shoot or a sprout, but it is something that has action to it: moving and growing. It is a "growing thing" and has the connotation of "abundant vitality and fresh life" (Leupold, p. 102). So what is this new living, growing phenomenon? Is it the beginning of the process of salvation for all mankind and for the heavens and the Earth as some interpret it, or is it a reference to the coming Messiah, Himself? Its thrust is like C. S. Lewis's description of the changes occurring in *Narnia*: "Aslan is on the move!" Let's not confuse this with the notion that the human condition is getting better and better. It is actually getting worse and worse, but there will come a time in the future when this glorious deliverance will come.

Covenant Theology, or its modern term Replacement Theology, teaches that the Church is now Israel, and all the blessings that were promised to Israel only apply to the Church. In a sense, Replacement Theology believes that the Kingdom is now, and any thought that there is a future for Israel does not exist. It teaches that the Kingdom of God is on Earth now, and spiritually, things are getting better and better. The concept of the *tsemach* (the Branch) being a living, transforming phenomenon, applies to our world right now. But as mentioned before, things are getting worse and worse, and we hope for the coming of the Messiah and His Kingdom. The *tsemach* can, however, refer to our personal relationship with the Lord and His ever-changing, life-giving presence in our lives as we walk with Him.

There are other references to the Messiah as a *shoot* or *branch*, but often the Hebrew word *netzer* is used. To add more to ponder, there are other words in Hebrew for *shoot* and *branch* as well. It was an agrarian society after all. We'll touch on this when we look at Isaiah Chapters 11 and 53.

Whatever position you take, it is mind boggling to think that throughout time, even in the darkest days, when persecution of Jewish people was paramount and suppression of sincere Christians was popular, there was still the great work of salvation manifesting in the lives of seeking souls. The *tsemach* is growing, gaining strength, about to become beautiful and glorious, about to bring tremendous deliverance for Israel and for the people of our Lord.

Verse 2 concludes with the proclamation that Israel will still survive. They will survive the coming Babylonian Captivity of Isaiah's time, and also survive the coming Tribulation period in the future "last days."

So, every verse does tell a story, and there are more stories to explore!

### Recorded for Life and Called Holy (Isaiah 4:3-4)

5/23/07

Let us continue in our study by looking at Isaiah 4, verses 3-4. In verse 3, those who will be left in Jerusalem, who are *recorded for life*, will be called *holy*. *Recorded for life* refers to the census records of the city at that time. However, this is a statement by the heavenly court proclaiming that the residents of Jerusalem at that future time will be called holy. Verse 4 references the fact that the filth and blood guilt of Israel's men and women will be *washed away* by the Lord via the spirit of judgment and the spirit of burning (Fruchtenbaum, cassette 2, side one). So God is doing the washing and cleansing. Israel has not accomplished this act in her own strength. At this time, Israel is turning to her Lord through a series of trials, and the Lord is cleansing and purifying her. If you reference Isaiah 53:1, you will see that Israel is astonished when she realizes who the Messiah is. *Who has believed our message? And to whom has the arm of the LORD been revealed?* In our terms, "Who would have believed it?!"

### Clouds by Day and Fire by Night (Isaiah 4:5-6)

In this new setting (verse 5) we see the Lord is once again present in Jerusalem as the *cloud by day, even smoke, and the brightness of a flaming fire by night*. Just as He guided Israel in the wilderness in Moses' time, so He will guide Israel in this future time. McClain describes the sad events of when the Glory of the Lord, the cloud and fire, departed from the Temple in Ezekiel's time, just before Babylon took over. He states, "We cannot fail to be impressed with the gracious circumstances of the LORD's withdrawal: not suddenly, but slowly and gradually by stages, with seeming tender reluctance, as if He were actually yearning to remain in the place He had chosen for His dwelling place" (p. 124).

McClain described these stages:

> First, the prophet Ezekiel saw the Glory still in the city of David in its proper place in the Temple (Ezekiel 8:4). A little later in the vision he notes that the Glory of the God of Israel was gone up ... *to the threshold of the temple* (Ezekiel 9:3). Then Ezekiel writes, *The Glory of the LORD .... stood over the threshold* (Ezekiel 10:4, King James Version). Finally, the cherubim lifted up their wings, and the prophet records the tragic end: *The Glory of the LORD went up from the midst of the city,*

*and stood upon the mountain which is east of the city* (Ezekiel 11:23) (pp. 123-124).

The Glory of the Lord, according to Fruchtenbaum (cassette 2, side one), returned again to Israel as the "star of Bethlehem" hovering over the birthplace of the Messiah. In the future we will see, according to Isaiah 4:5, the full return of the Glory of the Lord, the Shekinah Glory of Israel. *And there will be a shelter to give shade from the heat by day, and refuge and protection from the storm and the rain* (verse 6).

As for us, are we prepared to allow the Lord to cleanse us and be our shelter against the heat of the trials we face during the day, and a protection from the storms life presents at night? Or will we choose to go out on our own, thinking we can handle things ourselves?

More next time as we explore the vineyard of Isaiah Chapter 5.

# Isaiah Chapter 5   The Song of My Beloved Concerning His Vineyard

### 6/06/07

"I have just read Chapter 5." ___ yes

### God's Vineyard, The Perfect Parable (Isaiah 5: 1-5)

Isaiah Chapter 5 begins with these words from verse 1:

> *Let me sing now for my well-**beloved***
> *A song of my **beloved** concerning His vineyard.*
> *My well-**beloved** had a vineyard on a fertile hill.*
> [Bold emphasis is mine.]

Do you have a beloved, or are you the beloved? The word *beloved* can be a noun or an adjective. In Hebrew, the noun form is *dod*. According to Brown, Driver, and Briggs (p. 187), it means "loved one." *My beloved* in Hebrew is *dodi*. It is found here in Isaiah 5 and many times in the Song of Solomon. The adjective form in Hebrew is *yadid* (Brown, Driver, and Briggs, p. 391). It is translated here as "well beloved."

I love my wife and I want her to feel satisfied and fulfilled in all she does. She loves her gardens. When her fruit trees are getting blossoms, she is elated and looks forward to a bountiful harvest. She loves her roses, too, and knows how to take cuttings from her favorites and plant them in new locations to make more rose bushes! When one of them dies, she is crushed because she had put a lot of love and care into them and considers them her own. The following is a poem about another gardener, and you can see how the narrator feels when the beloved's vineyard did not produce good grapes even though everything possible was done to help them thrive:

> My beloved had a vineyard on a very fertile hill.
> He digged and cleared it all of stones, the land was good to till.
> He built a wine vat in its midst, and planted it with vines.
> He looked for it to yield good grapes that he might drink the wine.
>
> But as the fruit matured he saw how wild the grapes became.
> Although he loved and cared for them, the vine would not be tamed.
> Why children of Jerusalem did not the harvest yield?
> What more could my beloved do to tend his wasted field?
>
> The keeper of the vineyard, the Lord of Hosts is He.
> The vineyard is His people. Oh tell me can't you see.
> That He was seeking righteousness and justice for His wine.
> Instead He found iniquity hanging on the vine.
>
> For you who seek the Lord today, the lesson still holds true.
> For what He sought of Israel, He still requires of you.
> So walk with Him in righteousness, and be a fruitful vine,
> And press your life into His hands, that He might drink the wine.

Some of you may have recognized the above as the lyrics of "The Vineyard Song" written by Stuart Dauermann in the early 1970s. It depicts the spirit of the passage we are about to study in Isaiah Chapter 5, verses 1-7. The passage in Isaiah is a parable, and according to Leupold, "as to literary form, one of the most perfect parables of Scripture" (p. 108). In the parable, Isaiah "assumes the role of a sort of minstrel, or 'ballad singer.'" It may, for instance, have been presented at some public gathering or major festival (p. 108).

The topic, the vineyard, was a very common entity in the society during Isaiah's time, one that people could easily relate to. It was an attention getter. Just as Isaiah used an easily relatable metaphor to reach God's people, isn't it the personality of our Lord to relate to us in ways we can grasp? *Yeshua*, Jesus, used parables extensively in His ministry. He relayed them in a way that those who were sensitive to the deeper meaning of the parables could grasp them, and those who were not sensitive, could not. In my opinion, it was a beautiful and sensitive way to communicate. It was not high theology but was very down to earth and practical.

In my journeys, I found that I could use those very parables that Jesus taught to communicate deeper truths to those searching for answers. On one occasion I remember walking through a local open market in Mexico handing out literature and talking to people. There were fish laid out on ice for people to choose from, and being inspired by the Holy Spirit, I was able to talk to some merchants and say, "Jesus wants to make you fishers of men." I felt as if I were in biblical times.

### *Sometimes Our Hard Work Does not Produce Fruit (Isaiah 5:1-7)*

6/19/20

The concept of the vineyard is found not only in this passage in Isaiah 5; but it is also described in Jeremiah 2:21 and 12:10, Psalm 80:8, Matthew 21:33-46, Mark 12:1 and 2, and Luke 20:9-19. The story of the vineyard in Matthew, Mark, and Luke parallels almost word for word the beginning sequence of the Isaiah 5 passage.

Verses 1 and 2 give a description of the care put into forming this vineyard. It was planted on a fertile hill. The choice of soil was very carefully made. The word *fertile* gives the idea of "a son of oil" or "fatness" in Hebrew, according to Leupold. Being a hill, the vineyard was open to sunlight on all sides, an asset grapevines love (p. 110). The stones were removed. That's an accomplishment because stones are everywhere in that land (Fruchtenbaum, cassette 2, side one). Choice vines were planted, and a watchtower was constructed. The watchtower was centrally located to enable the watchman to guard against those who would pillage the vineyard. A wine vat was carved out of stone in anticipation of the harvest. However, as the end of verse 2 points out, instead of good grapes, the vineyard produced *worthless ones*, sour ones, stinking ones (Leupold, p. 110). So the narrator of the vineyard song asks the inhabitants of Judah, even Jerusalem, to judge between Him and His vineyard (verse 3), and then asks the question in verse 4, *"What more was there to do for My vineyard that I have not done in it?"*

Verse 5 continues with a "somewhat ominous ring" (Leupold, p. 111): *"So now let Me tell you what I am going to do to My vineyard: I will remove its hedge and it will be consumed; I will break down its wall and it will become trampled ground."* The hedge, as Leupold explains, "was often made of prickly pears in order to keep all manner of beasts from having easy access to the vines. The wall was usually made of stone" (p. 111). Its removal would allow the vineyard to become *"trampled ground."*

Verse 6 declares, *"And I will lay it waste."* The owner will see to it that the hill will become the equivalent of a gully, a precipitous place where nothing could grow. It will only have *"briars and thorns"* (Leupold, p. 111). The owner *"will also charge the clouds to rain no rain on it."* This looks pretty grim with no way out for Israel, but remember that God always preserves a remnant throughout the ages who do bear fruit, so to speak.

Writing carefully, Isaiah reveals the identity of the vineyard owner. Only the Almighty could command the clouds. The identity of the vineyard is also revealed in verse 7, *For the vineyard of the LORD of hosts is the house of Israel, and the men of Judah His delightful plant.*

Isaiah often likes to use a play on words and, as Leupold explains, employs this method again at the close of verse 7b (p. 112): *Thus he looked for justice [mishpat] but behold, bloodshed [mispach]; for righteousness [tsedaqah], but behold, a cry of distress [tse'aqah].* In our lives, what more could the Lord have done for us? He took upon Himself the brunt and penalty for our sin, and offers us freedom and forgiveness in exchange. He offers us eternal life and deliverance from the fear of death and also from fear of judgment. He took the judgment for us, on our behalf. All we need do is receive Him into our very being, and He will produce in us the rich and living fruit of the vine.

### *Oy Vay! (Isaiah 5:11-17)*
7/01/07

Isaiah Chapter 5 is more involved than I thought. This time we'll be looking at verses 11-17. The section begins with the word *woe*. In Hebrew the word is *hoi* and that is where we get the Yiddish word *oy*. So, the next time you hear your mother or neighbor's mother say, "Oy vay," at least you know how we got that term. In this chapter, the term appears in verses 8, 11, and 18 and in verses 20 through 22. *Oy vay.*

Verses 8-10 warn those who mistakenly follow the secular Golden Rule: "He who dies with the most toys wins." They can all go in a second. I remember talking to a woman who was the daughter of an immigrant from China. Her father was a successful businessman and acquired a great deal of wealth. Then communism swept through China; and, as if overnight, he lost everything he had built. He had nothing left. He then fled to the United States. Fortunately for him, as his daughter explained, he had his business in his head. He had no material wealth, but he took his business sense with him and was able to start again. Unfortunately, most were not as fortunate. Everything we have that is material can go away in a second. Yet, the Lord in our hearts will never leave us or forsake us.

The scene in verses 11 through 12 depicts a drinking party. What is striking to me is that, even though the description is more than 2500 years old, it seems nothing has changed, good or bad, from those times until now.

The people mentioned in verse 11 rose up early in the morning and stayed up late in the evening in their pursuit. A *pursuit* is defined as "an activity, such as a vocation or hobby, engaged in regularly" (*American Heritage College Dictionary,* p. 1132). Here the pursuit is strong drink and wine (verse 11).

Verse 12 continues, *And their banquets are accompanied by lyre and harp, by tambourine and flute, and by wine.* So, the people were eating and drinking and listening to music; it could have been loud or soft music. Regardless, the effect is the same. In my generation, we thought that rock, or hard rock, was the new thing and that our old folks listened to boring, uninspiring, listless music. What we didn't realize was that they thought their parents listened to dumb music too, and their parents thought the same of theirs. We may think flute and lyre and harp would put us to sleep, but to that generation and culture it was hot stuff; and it created the same emotional effect: "the escape." What is the escape? *They do not pay attention to the deeds of the LORD, nor do they consider the work of His hands* (verse 12). Leupold explains it this way, "The spirit of wine has dulled their senses to discern the presence of the Spirit of God" (p. 116).

It seems like what we pursue, what we put our minds to, is what we become. I was watching the famed movie classic, *Citizen Kane*. One of the characters, when describing Kane, said, "You can make a lot a money, if all you wanna do in life is make a lot a money." What is it that we are pursuing? What will be to our benefit in the long run?

> [13] *Therefore my people go into exile for their lack of knowledge; and their honorable men are famished, and their multitude is parched with thirst.*
> [14] *Therefore Sheol has enlarged its throat and opened its mouth beyond measure; and Jerusalem's splendor, her multitude, her din of revelry, and the jubilant within her, descend into it.*
> [15] *So the common man will be humbled, and the man of importance abased; the eyes of the proud also will be abased.*

In Hebrew, there are no capital letters. If a translator determines something is capital as opposed to lower case, it is based upon their interpretation of the passage. The New American Standard Bible, the Berean Standard Bible, the Amplified Bible, the Holman Christian

Standard Bible, and the *Tanakh: The Holy Scriptures* by the Jewish Publication Society all start verse 13 with *Therefore My people,* with the initial letter in *My* being capitalized. All the other commonly used versions I researched kept the *M* as lower case *m*. Even the commentators I looked at, Keil and Delitzsch, Leupold, and Ironside, keep the *m* as lower case. So the overwhelming position is that Isaiah, not God, is talking here.

Verse 13 uses the phrase, *Therefore **my** people.* With the use of the possessive *my,* Isaiah reveals his emotion and is not lacking in sympathy for *his people* who he knows will go into exile because of their lack of knowledge (Leupold, p. 116).

Surprisingly, there will be no distinction between their *honorable men* and the *multitude* (verse 13) because a great number of poor and rich will be lost in the judgment to come. In verse 14, the imagery is striking in that *Sheol has enlarged its throat and opened its mouth beyond measure. Sheol,* or the place of the dead, will enlarge its appetite, verse 14. Death will open its mouth without limit. The appetite of *Sheol,* the place of the dead, "will be so voracious that, in the process of feeding, she grows hungrier" (Leupold, p. 117).

Verse 15 continues, *The common man will be humbled, and the man of importance abased.* The pride of both groups will have left them. There is no favoritism, and both groups are treated equally. In our day, we have made the mistake of thinking that the rich are the bad guys and the poor are the good guys, or the well off and respected are the noble ones and favored by God while the poor are the lazy, slothful ones. As a social observation, both communism and fascism claimed to take the interests of the common man to heart, and positioned the elite of society as the reason for their societal woes. But the result of these political movements was indeed the height of evil. Keep in mind that God is the One who judges the thoughts and intents of the heart, and does not favor one section of society over another. In God's eyes, the little guy is as good, or as bad, as the big guy.

Verses 16 and 17 conclude the passage by explaining that *the LORD of hosts will be exalted in judgment* (verse 16), and it will be a fair and honorable judgment. If you have accepted Him, He has already taken the judgment for you. Concerning Israel, we saw in the parable of the vineyard that the land will become uninhabited and desolate. After God judges Israel, not as a parable but in reality, *lambs will graze as in their pasture, and strangers will eat in the waste places of the wealthy* (verse 17).

*Yeshua* reached out to the despised tax collector, the prostitute, and the blind, as well as the religious leaders of the day. His heart goes out to the orphan, the widow, and the poor; but His heart also goes out to the lonely, empty, and isolated rich. So let's choose our pursuit from the morning to the evening of each day to be instruments of God's compassion and life-giving truth. After all, you never know who may be seeking God, whatever their station in life.

### A Bunch of Woes, Many Oy's! (Isaiah 5:18-21)
7/15/07

We are now entering into the last two sections of Isaiah 5: verses 18-25 and 26-30. We won't have space or time to cover both here, so we'll have to put some off until the next installment. We'll focus on verses 18-21, which will give us a good taste of the troubles that lie ahead for Israel, and why.

Verse 18 begins with yet another *woe*. *Woe to those who drag iniquity with cords of falsehood, and sin as if with cart ropes.* Normally one puts the ropes on the horses, mules, or human slaves in order to pull the cart. In this case these individuals have put the cords upon themselves. They have willingly made themselves slaves. It was their free choice. What they are pulling is *falsehood.* They have chosen to believe a lie, and it has put them in bondage (Leupold, p. 118).

In verse 19, the words of those who mock God are revealed. They are saying, "If the Lord is real, let Him reveal Himself." That is a paraphrase, of course, but the attitude is a defiant one. *"Let the purpose of the Holy One of Israel draw near and come to pass, that we may know it!"* They are saying, "If God is at work, let Him make it apparent." In other words, "Show me a sign" (Leupold, p. 119).

I personally believe that if a person is truly seeking the Lord and asking for help in finding Him, the Lord will answer that prayer, though their prayer may be answered in a way unexpected. On the other hand, if one is not sincere and is brazen in one's challenge, the Lord will not comply. As Leupold explains, "They behave as though the Holy One of Israel had to be at their beck and call" (p. 119).

You see, the problem is that we have a very short memory. Some of us suffer from the disease called CRS, "can't remember stuff," in our daily lives. At the same time, we also have trouble remembering the countless blessings of God we've experienced all through our lives. How many times has that money come in just in time, or that job appeared out of nowhere? Can we remember the healing that happened unexpectedly that left the doctors baffled? How often have we been encouraged by someone who did not know our circumstances, and the words were spoken at just the right time? The children of Israel have had a history filled with deliverances. At times, the nation had seen God working in their lives with their eyes of faith; but at this time they were looking with eyes of unbelief.

Verse 20 records the next *woe*: *Woe to those who call evil good, and good evil, who substitute darkness for light and light for darkness, who substitute bitter for sweet and sweet for bitter!* Their perspective is all messed up. Their moral values no longer exist. There are no longer any absolutes. I was talking with a Jewish co-worker who believed that all faiths were valid and true for each individual. I challenged her with the possibility that what Hitler believed was valid and true for him, and was that okay with her? She got my point that there was a distinction between good and evil, and light and darkness.

The next *woe* is for *those who are wise in their own eyes, and clever in their own sight!* (verse 21). We often look at our belief in God from our own experience in life, not realizing that we are not the center of the universe. Whatever we experience, spiritually or emotionally, is the only truth we can accept. We need to realize that the source of truth is greater than we are and outside of ourselves. How many times have we talked with those who say, "I know this or that is true because the Lord revealed it to me"? No matter what you say, you can't change their minds, because their experience is greater than even the clear teaching of the Scripture.

### A Wildfire Is A-Coming (Isaiah 5:22-24)
7/23/07

We continue with Isaiah 5:22. *Woe to those who are heroes at drinking wine, and valiant men at mixing strong drink.* Here we get into the gut of the human soul when we see that men and women are bragging about how well they can mix various concoctions of drinks and boasting about how much alcohol they can consume.

When I was in high school I had a job at a bar, believe it or not. It lasted two days. I wasn't good at cleaning tables. I thought it was cool to watch how people mixed drinks. There was a swagger to it, a finesse. But apparently I didn't have that gift, so I pursued other interests. What a sad commentary about where people place values. In college, I remember a bunch of under-the-beer-influence students standing around a dorm throwing empty beer cans at the building. It was a kind of game. I remember thinking that there must be more to life than this.

Verse 23 continues, and you can insert right here an unwritten [*Woe to those*:] *Who justify the wicked for a bribe, and take away the rights of the ones who are in the right!* Corrupt judges! Sounds like today. Judges are supposed to represent the righteousness of God on earth. As Leupold says, "Judges are thought of in the Scriptures as the very men who represent the righteous God on earth and speak and judge in His name," but in this passage, "The upholders of righteousness themselves pervert righteousness" (p. 120).

So the judgment of God will eventually come (verse 24). It is described as a wildfire, a phenomenon all too familiar for Southern Californians. Using a Hebrew linguistic device, "both ends or extremes of an object are mentioned to describe the entire object" (Leupold, p.121). Here the extremes are the *root* and the *blossom. Therefore, as a tongue of fire consumes stubble, and dry grass collapses into the flame, so their* **root** *will become like rot and their* **blossom** *blow away as dust, for they have rejected the law of the LORD of hosts, and despised the word of the Holy One of Israel.* [Bold used to compare the extremes.]

I know we are upset about the Ten Commandments no longer being allowed in government facilities because of the concept of separation of church and state, and we may have felt threatened about the campaign to remove the phrase *In God We Trust* from our coinage, but I believe we have made these issues into sacred cows. We hope that by having the Ten Commandments in our courtrooms, God will be there too; but in reality, God had left the courtrooms long before the Ten Commandments were taken out. And we as a society really don't make God our trust. We make our money our trust. So what's the big deal? It's almost as if we're taking the Ark of the Covenant into battle assuming that God will be with us because we have the Ark. Having the Ten Commandments in our courtrooms may remind us of God's law and give us a sense of conviction, but it may be possible that God, Himself, has had enough of our double-mindedness as a nation.

Verse 25 concludes this section and introduces the agent of the coming judgment. In our next installment, we will see how the prophet Isaiah captures the emotion and vivid description of the power and awe of the advancing Assyrian army.

### God's Hand Is Still Stretched Out (Isaiah 5:25-30)

8/11/07

I used to attend *Beth Sar Shalom* meetings on Long Island in the early '70s. *Beth Sar Shalom* means the "House of the Prince of Peace." The meetings were at the home of Clara and Joe Rubin, both workers with The American Board of Missions to the Jews (ABMJ), now known as Chosen People Ministries International. The teacher was a Jewish guy named Marty, and – even though it was some 35 years ago – I still remember him teaching about the hand of the Lord being *stretched out still.* He taught that the Lord was still reaching out His hand to us in compassion while in the midst of judgment, calling us back to Him.

It is good to note that the Hebrew word for *stretch*, *natah*, seems to indicate the manifestation of God's power and influence whether in judgment or in deliverance. For example, in the early chapters of Exodus, God instructed Moses and Aaron to *stretch out your staff,* or *your rod,* or *stretch out your hand* when the plagues were sent to the Egyptians. When the people of Israel were pinned up against the Red Sea, with the awful sound of Egyptian chariots approaching, the Lord said to Moses, *"Lift up your staff and stretch out your hand over the sea and divide it, and the sons of Israel shall go through the midst of the sea on dry land."* Later, He said to Moses, *"Stretch out your hand over the sea so that the waters may come back over the Egyptians, over their chariots and their horsemen"* (Exodus 14:16, 26).

Sometimes in our lives, we need the Lord to stretch out His hand on our behalf. We may feel we are at the edge of the Red Sea with nowhere to turn. Sometimes the Lord puts us in those very situations so that we can witness His manifestation of power and deliverance.

So, verse 25 of Isaiah Chapter 5 explains that because they *despised the word of the Holy One of Israel* (verse 24), *He has stretched out His hand against* [His people] *and struck them down.* The verse also says, *His anger is not spent, but His hand is still stretched out.*

Look at the contrast. In Moses' time, the hand of the Lord was stretched out against the Egyptians, in deliverance of Israel. Here in Isaiah, the hand of the Lord is stretched out against Israel via the coming Assyrian invasion.

As Leupold explains,

> The description of the approaching Assyrian war machine is terrifying. They are coming swiftly (verse 26). Every soldier is at the peak of physical condition, well fed and rested. Their arrows are sharp and their bows are bent. The horses are in prime shape and even their hooves are described as made of flint. The wheels of the chariots are seen as whirlwinds (verses 27, 28). The shout of the army is said to have the terror of the roaring of a lion (verse 29). And verse 30 concludes the chapter by describing the emotion of Israel, in that only darkness was above them and below them, as if alone at sea. (p. 123)

In contrast, and as a deliverance of sorts, Chapter 6 shows Isaiah in the presence of the brilliance of the glory of the Lord. We will look at Isaiah's vision in the Temple next time.

# Isaiah Chapter 6 "Whom Shall I Send?"

8/20/07

"I have just read Chapter 6." ___ yes

### Before and After (Isaiah 6:1-3)

Isaiah 6 starts with the phrase: *In the year of King Uzziah's death*. I like the way the New American Standard Bible translates this phrase because we do not know if Isaiah saw the following vision before Uzziah died or after he died. The King James Version translates it: *In the year that King Uzziah died,* giving some the impression that Isaiah 6 was written after Uzziah's death, which occurred around 742 BCE; so we may look at this dating as a reference point (Leupold, p. 126). It would be akin to saying: "In the same year that Kennedy was assassinated" or "the same year that World War II began."

A question arises when we consider that Isaiah was recording the time frame of his call to the ministry as a prophet of God. Some say that the passage should have been placed at the beginning of his prophesy as the true Isaiah Chapter 1. Others say that the content of the chapter really flows with the theme of God's judgment and rightfully belongs as a continuation of Chapters 2 – 5 (Leupold, p. 126). I personally see the opening verses of the chapter as a reflection of his past, or in modern terms, as a flashback. It could have been placed here as a support for why Isaiah was speaking so harshly toward his people.

We do not know if Isaiah's experience in the presence of God was a vision, a dream, or actual. The possibility that Isaiah was actually in God's presence is doubtful because he could not have looked at God's face and lived (Leupold, p. 128). In Exodus 33:20, Moses wanted to see God's glory, but the Lord said to Moses, *"You cannot see My face, for no man can see Me and live!"*

So what did Isaiah see? He saw *the Lord sitting on a throne, lofty and exalted, with the train of His robe filling the temple* (Isaiah 6:1). Leupold described it as the sweeping length of His robe (p. 129). Maybe the position of the throne was similar to the one in Solomon's Temple. Solomon's Temple had six steps going up to the throne, with two lion carvings or statues placed on each side of each step (1 Kings 10:18-20).

The *seraphim*, or flame-like beings, or burning ones that Isaiah saw, *stood above Him* (verse 2). The *im* ending of *seraphim* is a masculine plural ending. You can refer to one *seraph* or two or three *seraphim*, and they would all be male. It would not be correct to say, "He saw the *seraphims*," as that would have two plural endings, the first one in Hebrew (*im*) and an additional one in English (*s*).

This brings up an interesting side note because the word for God in Genesis Chapter 1 is *Elohim*. *El* is the root for God, and the *im* ending indicates the masculine plural. Such would logically suggest that God is a plurality and would give support for the idea of a triune God, or the Trinity.

Each *seraph* has six wings: two covering his face, two covering his feet, and two with which to fly. A *seraph* has human features, and the gestures of covering his face and feet reflect his humility toward God. According to Leupold, the *seraphim* reflect the holiness of God (p. 130).

Verse 3 shows us that the *seraphim* are calling *"Holy, Holy, Holy."* They are praising antiphonally, or in a reciprocal exchange. They are calling one to another. One calls, and another calls in return. Leupold suggests that the song goes on uninterruptedly and the *seraphim* especially rejoice in extolling God's holiness (p. 130).

Why do the *seraphim* say *Holy* three times? We'll look at that next time!

### Two's Company; Three's a Triunity (Isaiah 6:3)
9/14/07

Isaiah Chapter 6 is proving to be a most astounding chapter. I honestly had a hard time writing this latest study because the holiness of God is so convicting; and I, too, would have to live up to what the chapter teaches.

In our last study, we discussed that the *seraphim* were calling *Holy, Holy, Holy* back and forth among themselves (verse 3). And now, may I ask the question as to why the *seraphim* use the word *Holy* three times? Some say it is because it shows the superlative, a term showing the highest value out of three or more persons or things. In English, the superlative form of an adjective indicates the greatest of three or more things being described. On the other hand, comparative adjectives only compare two items. Examples of the superlative are *biggest, highest*, or *greatest*. Examples of the comparative are *bigger, higher,* or *greater*. So we say, "My computer is *faster* than your computer," using the comparative when comparing two like items. However, out of three or more items being compared in value, we say, "His computer is the *fastest,*" using the superlative adjective.

So let us get back to the question of why the *seraphim* say *"Holy, Holy, Holy"* regarding God. Why not just say it one or two times? One may be *holier* than another, the comparative; but God is *holiest* of all, the superlative. When using the adverbs *more* and *most*, the notion that God is the superlative in holiness has merit. Consider the phrase, "The Most High God" rather than saying "The More High God," with *More* being the comparative but *Most* being the superlative.

In our language and maybe in others as well, we tend to think in threes. Every conversation has three parts: an introduction, a middle, and a conclusion. Every sermon seems to have three points. We use the terms, *small, medium,* and *large* when ordering drinks or pizza. Ovens have low, medium, and high settings. Steaks can be prepared as rare, medium, or well done. Every object has a height, width, and depth. $H_2O$ comes as ice, water, or steam. There are many other examples, but what I am suggesting is that maybe it has significance in that our Creator's nature is in threes also. Perhaps the *seraphim* were singing *Holy, Holy, Holy* because God is a triune God, or a Tri-unity.

The Jewish concept of God is that God is one and not three. The prayer recited in the synagogue every week is *"Shema Yisrael Adonai Elohenu Adonai echad." "Hear, O Israel! The LORD is our God, the LORD is one!"* (Deuteronomy 6:4). *Echad* does mean "one, one of something"; but there are also times when *echad* means "a united *one.*" For example, Genesis 2:24 says: *For this cause a man shall leave his father and his mother, and shall cleave to his wife; and the two shall become **one** flesh.* The word here for *one* is *echad* – where two become one in essence and unity.

In this sense, we are saying that God is three persons in essence and unity and yet remains one God. The Trinity, so to speak, is not three separate gods, but one God comprised of three persons, a Tri-unity.

To help us understand this, we can use the illustration of height, width, and depth mentioned earlier. If you have a box that has height, width, and depth, and you take away the height, you will have no box left. If you take away the width, you also will have no box; the box will not exist. If you take away the depth, you also will have the same result.

In the same way – and please allow me to respectfully use this illustration – the triune God is Father, Son, and Spirit. If you take away the Father, there will no longer be the Son and the Spirit. If you take away the Son, there will no longer be the Father and the Spirit. If you take away the Spirit, you will no longer have the Father and the Son.

Granted, from our perspective, it is impossible to fully grasp this concept.

Moving on, Isaiah's experience brings up a troubling thought. Isaiah is experiencing the supernatural, the paranormal. He has seen and heard a view from heaven. Some people have never experienced the supernatural, and look at it as mythology and superstition. They believe only in logic and natural science. Others have experienced the paranormal to some degree via house spirits, white or black witchcraft, or encounters with forms of energy of light and darkness. Things happen around their house or dwelling that they cannot explain otherwise. Some see and hear the paranormal. So, for these individuals, their worldview includes the existence of a spirit world. Yet many who have experienced the spirit world still have trouble believing that there could be a God who does exist and who loves them. If one believes in a spirit world outside of our natural world, why can't they accept the existence of God and His angels as part of this spirit world? Why is a concept such as this so difficult to accept?

### *Too Loud – Too Old (Isaiah 6:4-5)*

9/23/07

Isaiah was in the presence of the holiness of God. How fitting to complete this study just after the observance of Yom Kippur, the Day of Atonement. It is the holiest day of the Jewish calendar. We see that Chapter 6, verse 4, continues the theme of holiness: *the foundations of the thresholds trembled at the voice of him who called out, while the temple was filling with smoke.* I usually complain that the bass guitar is too loud on our worship team because its vibrations overpower the stage where I'm playing my simple little mandolin. A friend of mine admonished me by saying, "Too loud – too old." In other words, if I thought the music was too loud, I was too old. Isaiah experienced the whole foundation of the doorways shaken at the resonance of the voices of the *seraphim*. Leupold (p. 132) described it this way, "Isaiah could experience the powerful reverberations caused by the mighty song of the *seraphim*. How majestic and powerful this great hymn was, and how impressive."

What could the smoke in verse 4 be? Well three suggestions are presented. It could be the cloud of the Shekinah Glory, the cloud seen by day and the pillar of fire seen at night during the Exodus. It could be the smoke rising from the altar when incense was placed on its live coals. Or it could be an image of God's wrath as illustrated in Psalm 18:7 (Leupold, pp. 132-133). See Psalm 18:7-8 for the dramatic picture this passage paints of God's anger:

*⁷ Then the earth shook and quaked;*
*And the foundations of the mounts were trembling*
*And were shaken, because He was angry.*

*⁸ Smoke went up out of His nostrils,*
*And fire from His mouth devoured;*
*Coals were kindled by it.*

Verse 5 continues with Isaiah's reaction: *Then I said, "Woe is me, for I am ruined! Because I am a man of unclean lips, and I live among a people of unclean lips; for my eyes have seen the King, the LORD of hosts."* Other translators have recorded Isaiah's reaction as, *"I am lost," "I am undone,"* or *"I am dissolved."* In essence, "I have become as nothing before You." Leupold's translation was: *"I am ruined"* (p. 133).

While Isaiah was immediately aware of his own shortcomings, he was also concerned for his people. I guess it's a lesson for us all to watch what we say with our mouths, whether gossip, harsh words, cursing, hurtful communications, and things we wish – in hindsight – that we could have taken back. As our Lord put it, it's *"not what enters into the mouth that defiles the man,"* referring to eating only kosher foods, *"but what proceeds out of the mouth, this defiles the man"* (Matthew 15:11). And it is the burden of the prophet of God to not only be burdened for the prophet's own spiritual welfare, but to be overwhelmed with the spiritual condition of the people.

Being a prophet was not a desired position or office. We do not see those called going willingly. The hesitancy expressed by Isaiah and other biblical prophets is in contrast to the modern day Prophetic movement where people jump at the opportunity to pretend they are in the same position of responsibility and office as those who were called in biblical times.

## "Depart from Me for I Am a Sinful Man, Oh Lord!" (Luke 5:8) – (Isaiah 6:5-6)
### 9/30/07

The more you know, the less you know. The more you know, the more you realize how much you don't know. When I first started playing guitar, I thought I was an acceptable guitar player. I played basic chords, and even bar chords. Then I realized there were minor seventh, diminished, and augmented chords. There were also many scales to learn, and I began to ponder how many years it would take to become an accomplished classical guitarist. Not only that, but the guitar itself needs consideration. You need to think about the quality of wood and whether or not the neck has inner support to prevent it from warping, the quality of the strings, and whether or not the guitar has sustain, which means how long the sound can play before dying out.

It's the same way with our relationship to the Lord. When I was a young believer, I thought I was good. I didn't drink, chew, or smoke.

My friend once asked me, "Do you drink?"

I said, "I sure do."

He said, "Alcohol!?"

I replied, "No, I drink water, juice, and milk."

I was good. The bad people were bad. As I had mentioned before, I had tremendous needs. When I asked *Yeshua* into my heart and life, I began to see areas that needed healing. I was stubborn, prideful, arrogant, and my close family members would refer to me as abrupt. I remember talking to a member of the *Liberated Wailing Wall*, the Jews

For Jesus musical group in the early 1970s, who said to me, "You're a good brother, Harry; but you have to be broken."

Slowly, but surely, the Spirit of the Lord was working in my heart. In time, I realized that I could not admit my shortcomings until I could understand God's love for me. I could not understand my sinfulness until I could compare it to His holiness. It's this relationship with the Lord, the give and take and the trust that gives us the ability to share our failures and mistakes with the Lord, knowing that He – at the same time – understands our weaknesses and willingly forgives us. He is happy when we honestly share with Him our brokenness and needs, and He wants to walk with us in a continually renewed relationship.

Once again, as we look at Chapter 6, verse 5; we see the profound effect that God's appearance had on Isaiah. He exclaimed: *"I am a man of unclean lips, and I live among a people of unclean lips; for my eyes have seen the King, the LORD of hosts."* Notice that Isaiah compared his speech to that of the *seraphim*. Their mouths were filled with praise, and he could see that his lips were not as sanctified. As Fruchtenbaum asserts in his tape series on Isaiah, "It's only when we can see God's holiness that we can appreciate our own sinfulness" (cassette 2, side two). When we compare ourselves to others, we can say we are okay or we're not all that bad; but all of us, when compared to the holiness of God, will fall way short. Fruchtenbaum cites the example found in the Book of Job where, compared to his friends, Job came out pretty good; but in the last four chapters, when Job encountered God, he became speechless (cassette 2, side two).

Isaiah 6:6-7 continues, *Then one of the seraphim flew to me, with a burning coal in his hand which he had taken from the altar with tongs. And he touched my mouth with it and said, "Behold, this has touched your lips; and your iniquity is taken away, and your sin is forgiven."* The *seraph* touched the area of Isaiah's weakness: his speech. It is interesting here to observe that "the *seraph* acts as a priest would act functioning at the altar" (Leupold, p. 135). As mentioned earlier in our study of this chapter, we do not know if Isaiah's experience in the presence of God was a vision or dream or actual. We do know that "burning" symbolizes purification. The nature of the cleansing is a matter of debate.

All in all, it is good for us to accept the cleansing that God provides through Messiah because we cannot enter heaven on our own merit. We're simply not good enough to get there even though our intentions may be completely sincere.

Next time we will finish Chapter 6 by looking at the nature of God's throne room and royal court and the nature of God, Himself. We will also examine Isaiah's calling to the ministry and the results of his ministry. Such will give hope for any of us who may be discouraged because we think we are not having a successful ministry!

### *Hineni: Here I Am! (Isaiah 6:8-9)*

10/14/07

As we continue, Isaiah had witnessed God's throne room and God's holiness. The Lord then asked the question, *"Whom shall I send, and who will go for Us?"* (verse 8). Isaiah replied, *"Here am I. Send me!"* Isaiah was not in a position where he could say "no" to God. He would not have time to say, "Let me pray about it" or "Give me some time to consider this." Sometimes God calls us, and we know that we have to say "yes" to His call.

I remember being speechless in 1971 after hearing a reply from a faithful Christian lady. I had asked her, "Don't you think Jesus is a crutch, and don't you think weak people come to Him because they need something to hang on to for a while?" As she smiled at me, her reply was, "Of course!" I had never heard that before. I always thought God was up there somewhere, a benevolent heavenly Father figure; but I never thought He was concerned for the small details of my life and for my needs.

You see, I had worked as a volunteer at a cerebral palsy camp the summer before. While we were working with the kids by the pool, a preacher, a religious fanatic, came to the camp and was preaching to us about Jesus. He looked at me and said, "I know you believe." I wouldn't have said I believed but that I was sensitive to what he was saying. After he left, one of the counselors, whom I knew to be very popular and a great athlete, said, "I can't understand why there would be a God if He would allow people to have cerebral palsy." But then, one of the girls who had CP started yelling at him as best she could, saying, "No, no, God is real, God is real!" So, it was apparent that the girl who had CP believed in God with all her heart; but the well-to-do counselor did not believe at all. She had the need, and she believed; whereas, the counselor, who had everything going for him, did not believe at all.

So this godly woman asserted that God is deeply concerned for us and can be our crutch. After hearing this simple woman's reply to my kind of arrogant question, I knew God was calling me. I knew He had understood my observations at the CP camp from the year before. He also understood that I had tremendous needs. My whole concept of God had changed at that very moment. He was speaking directly to me, and I had no other option but to receive Him into my life.

God's question to Isaiah was, *"Who will go for Us?"* This is another instance in Isaiah that suggests that God is a plurality, where

God the Father is talking to the other members of the Godhead: God the Son, and God the Holy Spirit. Others prefer to believe in this particular case in Isaiah 6 that God is referring to His heavenly court with the use of the term *Us*. Leupold states, "God is represented for human understanding after the manner of a monarch of this earth who sits upon a throne and has a royal court (an angelic court) in attendance" (p. 136). The presence of a royal court can also be found in the early chapters of Job and in 1 Kings 22:19 where the prophet Micaiah is testifying: *"I saw the LORD sitting on His throne, and all the host of heaven standing by Him on His right and on His left"* (Leupold, p. 136).

This use of the first person plural (we, us, our) is also presented in Genesis 1:26 where it states, *"Let Us make man in Our image, according to Our likeness."* In the Genesis account, though, it is not plausible to say that God is talking to His angels because man is not made in the image and likeness of angels.

Isaiah was told that the people he would be ministering to would not believe his message (verses 9 and 10). Isaiah's message from God to Israel was, *"'Keep on listening, but do not perceive; keep on looking, but do not understand'"* (Isaiah 6:9b). He was being called to an unsuccessful ministry. Fruchtenbaum (cassette 2, side two) mused that Isaiah would not be able to write in his prayer letters about how many people would come to the Lord. In a way, it's an encouragement for those who are dealing with groups not receptive to the good news.

I had a dream last night that different people were living in some kind of care facility. We could visit people when we wanted, but sometimes some people would disappear. It was explained to me that they had only a certain time to believe; and if their time expired, they would no longer be there. It is true that God gives each individual a period of time to consider His claims; and when that time has expired, that person's heart will start to harden. It's like a window of opportunity. It happened with Pharaoh in the Book of Exodus. Each time he resisted Moses' message to *"Let my people go,"* Pharaoh's heart was hardened more, until he could no longer believe. So we continue to pray that people's eyes would be opened and their ears would be able to hear the good news and find life in Messiah.

In verse 11, Isaiah asked the question, *"Lord, how long?"* The Lord's answer was, according to Ironside: "The message must be proclaimed until there were none left to hear" (p. 42). To break it down, verse 11 continues: *"Until cities are devastated and without inhabitant, houses are without people, and the land is utterly desolate."* Verse 12 states: *"The LORD has removed men far away, and the forsaken places are many in the midst of the land."* Leupold says on page 140, Israel and Judah must go into captivity.

In verse 13, according to Leupold, the nation of Israel will be brought down to a level where only a tenth of the residents are left in the land. Even that will not be the end of what shall befall. That tenth shall again be burned. A nation could hardly be brought lower and still be called a nation. The illustration shows that a significant tree was cut down, but its stump still remained. The stump is left, but it is not dead. The last line in verse 13 says, *"The holy seed is its stump."* According to Keil and Delitzsch (p. 132), "The root stump could shoot out and put forth branches again .... The root stump was the remnant that had survived the judgment and would become a seed out of which a new Israel would spring up after the old had been destroyed." So in the midst of despair, the Lord always gives hope.

Next time we will venture into Chapter 7 and discuss the historical background and context of the famous Messianic passage contained in verse 14: *"Behold, a virgin will be with child and bear a son, and she will call His name Immanuel"* which means "God with us."

# Isaiah Chapter 7 "Ask for a Sign"

11/01/07

"I have just read Chapter 7." ___ yes

### The Freedom to Question (Isaiah 7:1, 14)

Being a young Jewish believer, it was easy to accept numerous passages as being Messianic, referring to the coming Messiah, without questioning whether they actually were or not. Later in my faith, I began to question what I had been taught and found that, indeed, some passages were taken out of context. I then grew disappointed and discouraged, and I felt manipulated. In other words, the lesson I learned was to examine the whole context of a passage in order to find the meaning of a passage.

As a side note, I have found the Ryrie Study Bible to be a reliable source when examining the Scriptures. Ryrie doesn't try to make something out of what isn't. Also, I recommend the *Daily Bible Experience*. It's a 365-day, chronologically-arranged New International Version resource, with commentary by F. LaGard Smith. He offers historical explanations that are very easy to follow. I have also noticed that he seems sensitive to Jewish issues and avoids terms that may be offensive to Jewish readers.

Isaiah Chapter 7, the fourteenth verse, had been one of those troubling passages for me. When looking at the verse alone, sure, the evidence is quite convincing that it is referring to the virgin birth of the Messiah: *"Therefore the Lord Himself will give you a sign: Behold, a virgin will be with child and bear a son, and she will call His name Immanuel"* (which means "God with us"). However, when looking at the verses around this one, it didn't make much sense to me to say the passage was Messianic.

You see, the argument has always centered on the Hebrew word *almah* and whether it meant "a young maiden" or "a virgin." The Jewish stand has traditionally been that the word *betulah* meant "virgin," and *almah* was simply a young woman and not necessarily a virgin. So Jewish scholars would say that if Isaiah wanted to say, "A virgin would conceive and bear a son," he would have used *betulah*. Then, they would ask what kind of sign it would be if a young woman gave birth to a child! That would simply be part of life.

In contrast, using the same logic, a young woman giving birth would not be much of a sign; but a virgin giving birth would! Note that the *Septuagint*, the Greek translation of the Hebrew Scriptures – which was completed in Alexandria, Egypt, and dates from the third century BCE – translates the word *almah* as "parthenos," which specifically means "virgin." Also, in the Hebrew Publishing Company's English translation of The Holy Scriptures (1936), we get some additional insight from the Song of Solomon. In Chapter 1, verse 3, and in Chapter 6, verse 8, the word *alamot* (feminine plural for almah) is translated as "virgins"; and yet in Isaiah 7:14, their translation of *almah* is still "young woman." So inconsistency in translating the same word does exist.

Later in my life, upon studying the passage further, I found that verse 7:14 does indeed fit nicely and logically within the context of the preceding verses. In order to see this perspective, one needs to examine the historical sequence of events that led up to verse 14.

## A Deeper Look (Isaiah 7:1-3)
11/15/07

As we continue in our study of Isaiah Chapter 7, I noted that the issue of the *virgin birth* mentioned in verse 14 could be supported by the context of the verses preceding it. At that time, about 735 BCE, the Assyrians had taken Israel (the northern kingdom) and had also taken Syria. Israel and Syria wanted to revolt against Assyria. So what did they do? They attacked Judah (the southern kingdom) with the logic that their aggression would force Judah into an alliance with them against their common aggressor Assyria. At the very least, upon Judah's defeat, they could place a puppet king on the Judean throne instead of Ahaz. The king of Syria was Rezin, and the king of Israel at that time was Pekah. The proposed puppet king was called "the son of Tabeel." He was an unknown person and a collaborator (Leupold, p. 150).

So, verse 1 is an overview of the following verses, introducing the main characters:

Ahaz, the son of Jotham, the son of Uzziah, king of Judah

Rezin the king of Aram (Syria)

Pekah, the son of Remaliah, king of Israel

And verse 1 describes how the king of Israel and the king of Syria attempted to conquer Jerusalem but couldn't. The verses following play out some of the details referred to in Isaiah's introductory overview.

Verse 2 mentions the House of David. Remember this reference as we continue throughout the passage:

*When it was reported to the House of David, saying, "The Arameans have camped in Ephraim," his heart*

> [the heart of Ahaz] *and the hearts of his people shook as the trees of the forest shake with the wind.*

When they learned the intentions of Rezin and Pekah to attack Jerusalem, everyone in the southern kingdom went on high alert because the enemy was only a 3-day journey away! Leupold mentioned that each one of the two forces alone was stronger than Judah at that time (p. 148).

I remember when I was in seminary in the mid 1970s. Arafat, the notorious founder of the Palestinian Liberation Organization, had just spoken at the U.N., and a newspaper picture showed him with both arms raised. You could see he had an olive branch in one hand and you could also see, on his other side, a gun sitting in his jacket pocket. At that moment I experienced a fear I had never felt before. I literally shook. All the security I had, living in the U.S.A., seemed to vanish before me as I realized that the U.N. would let such a monster address the General Assembly. It took a lot of prayer from friends, and also personal counseling, in order to understand why I was so fearful. Ultimately I learned I was depending on the security of my family and the strength of our country more than the strength of our Lord. I wasn't able to grasp His love at that time; but in time, I grew in faith.

If we are honest, I think most of us have had a time of tremendous fear. Do not take it as a defeat. Take it as a learning process to help you understand your God-given emotions. Look at it as a way to learn more of God's power on your behalf in the midst of trial, and as a way to understand more of His love and compassion for you and yours.

Verse 3 reveals that Isaiah was then commissioned by the Lord to meet Ahaz in order to encourage him. The verse reads, *Then the LORD said to Isaiah, "Go out now to meet Ahaz, you and your son*

*Shear-jashub."* Isn't it interesting that Isaiah refers to himself in the third person? It should have read, *Then the LORD said to me.* It's fascinating to me that Isaiah had the confidence to bring his 3-year-old son with him to meet Ahaz. At that time, Ahaz was at the conduit of the upper pool, checking the water supply of the city in anticipation of an attack.

Isaiah's message, as taken verbatim from God, was to *"'take care, and be calm, have no fear and do not be fainthearted'"* (verse 4). We'll find out why next time!

## "The Only Thing We Have to Fear Is Fear Itself"
### (Franklin D. Roosevelt) (Isaiah 7:4-12)

11/23/07

Well, I left you hanging last time, so now we must continue. Isaiah's message to Ahaz was: "Watch yourself and keep calm!" (Leopold's translation of verse 4, p. 146). "Nothing was to be done rashly on impulse or out of panic" (p. 149). The reason was because Rezin and Pekah were *"'smoldering firebrands'"* (verse 4). In California we are deluged with wildfires because of strong Santa Ana winds. After the fires go through, all that is left are the charred remains of trees and brush, in other words, smoking firebrands. Rezin and Pekah had no power left. Their fire was already extinguished. "Smoke may emanate, but [it] can do no damage" (Leupold, p. 149). Isaiah touches on this theme later in his prophesy when he writes, *Behold, the nations are like a drop from a bucket, and are regarded as a speck of dust on the scales; behold, He lifts up the islands like fine dust* (Isaiah 40:15).

Rezin and Pekah's plan, as described in verses 5 and 6, was first to fill Judah and Jerusalem with fear via a war of words. Then their plan was to split Judah in half, and finally to set up the puppet king, the Son of Tabeel. Who was this mysterious character? No one seems to know. We do know he was a Syrian and had a good Syrian name. Isaiah often makes a play on words; and, according to Leupold, Isaiah incorporated a slightly altered spelling of the word "Tabeel" to mean "good for nothing." We also know that this character would not be from the line of Judah (Leupold, p. 150).

It's safe to say that it was of great concern for Ahaz that Judah's line would be preserved because the future Messiah was to be from the line of Judah. Remember how, in verse 2, the news of the impending invasion was reported to the "House of David"? Messiah will be a "son of David" and will sit on the "throne of David." The Son of Tabeel, set up as the king of Judah, would not meet these qualifications.

Over the ages, Satan has repeatedly tried to destroy the Messianic line. If Pharaoh had had his way, Moses would have been one of those murdered when the decree came that all newly born Hebrew males should be thrown into the Nile River. If Herod had his way, *Yeshua* would have been slaughtered during his campaign to rid the Bethlehem area of male children ages 2 and under. Looking to our future, Antichrist will play the role of the puppet king in Jerusalem. So, as you can see, this Son of Tabeel has more significance than we may have thought at first.

Verses 7-9 continue: Rezin is the King of Damascus "only," and not of Judah. Pekah is the head of Israel "only" and no more. They may aspire to be more, but their plan will not come to pass. They also will have a limited future (Leupold, pp. 150-151). Although the outcome was not clear to Ahaz yet, Isaiah clearly prophesied that God, Himself, stated, *"It shall not stand nor shall it come to pass."*

In verses 10-12, the Lord asked Ahaz to ask for a sign to reassure him that God was with Judah, but Ahaz refused to ask because he did not want to *test the LORD*. We'll explore this exchange next time!

### *I Will Not Ask (Isaiah 7:10-12)*
12/10/07

Starting at verse 10 of Isaiah 7 and continuing through verse 12, the text reads: *Then the LORD spoke again to Ahaz saying, "Ask a sign for yourself from the LORD your God, make it deep as Sheol or high as heaven."* In response, Ahaz said, *"I will not ask, nor will I test the LORD!"*

Well, Ahaz didn't want to put the Lord to the test, but when God proposes a sign in which to invest one's faith, one is not putting God to the test. Ahaz could have asked a sign from the depths of *Sheol* and the underworld to the highest of heaven. If Ahaz did accept the sign, he would be under obligation to believe the sign (Leupold, p. 154).

Ahaz's agenda may not have coincided with God's agenda. Maybe he wanted to deliver Judah his own way by trusting in Assyria for help. His attitude was seemingly humble, yet underneath were signs of stubbornness and pride. Leupold put it this way, "The pious sound of his answer masks a very stubborn unbelief" (p. 155).

Ahaz gave a clever answer that was non-committal. It reminds me of the parable Jesus taught about the man going on a journey (Matthew 25:14-30). As the man was leaving, he entrusted to one slave 5 talents, to one 2 talents, and to another 1 talent, in order to bring back a profit. According to Walvoord in his book *Thy Kingdom Come* (pp. 197-198), a talent was a large sum of money, varying greatly in value according to whether it was silver or gold, and could weigh from 58 to 80 pounds. Walvoord projected that by 1974 a "gold talent could be worth as much as $30,000." The value of 80 pounds of gold today is about $2.5 million. The one who had 5 talents ($12.5 million) brought back 10 (in today's terms, as much as $25 million). The one who had 2 talents ($5 million) came back with twice as much ($10 million). However, the one who had one talent hid the money and simply returned the talent back to his master. He said he was afraid of losing what he had. This one was being clever in his own eyes, but in reality he did not want to commit to trusting in the Lord.

So, if God has given you a gift, use it and don't be afraid of messing up. Step out, and God will help you because He appreciates our taking the step for Him.

Anyway, back to our text. Ahaz's reply was frustrating for Isaiah and for God as well. Leupold (p. 155) asserts, "The King's vacillation and inability to take a wholesome attitude is a severe trial for God, Himself."

Isaiah was so upset with Ahaz's neither-hot-nor-cold attitude that he said, in verse 13, *"Is it too slight a thing for you to try the patience of men, that you will try the patience of my God as well?"* With the phrase *patience of my God,* Isaiah affirmed that the Lord was Isaiah's God, but also suggested that Ahaz didn't really have a God. Leupold said that the word *my* "appears to have been spoken with some vehemence and with a justifiable measure of impatience" (p. 155).

So what was the sign for unbelieving Ahaz? Isaiah Chapter 7, verse 14 tells us that God chose the sign: *"A virgin will be with child and bear a son, and she will call His name Immanuel."* Ahaz did not have the insight, but it seems that Isaiah did. In the future, a virgin will give birth to a descendent of Judah and David. This was said to assure Ahaz that the Messianic line will be preserved. The *son of Tabeel* will not gain the throne of the House of David in Jerusalem. The child who will be born will be "God with us," signified by His name, *Immanuel*. This mysterious child appears again in Isaiah Chapter 8, verses 8 and 10; Isaiah Chapter 9, verse 6; and Chapter 11, verse 1.

From Ahaz's perspective, the child named Immanuel will be born in the here and now. The child will not be able to eat the normal diet of meats, vegetables, and grains. He will eat "curds and honey" because, even at his small age, Jerusalem and Judah will be under siege, and all that will be available to eat will be the aforementioned minimal diet (verse 15). Before the boy will be able to discern the morality of good and evil, he will know the physical effects of good and evil as a child in a land under siege.

Oftentimes we can look at our surroundings and say that things are okay, or when going through tremendous trials, that things are not okay. But if we could look at things from God's perspective, we may be surprised at how He's working in our lives and in the lives of those we love. We'll begin Chapter 8 next time!

# Isaiah Chapter 8   Do Not Fear What They Fear

1/02/08

"I have just read Chapter 8." ___ yes

### Immanuel, Continued (Isaiah 8:1-4)

To my surprise, Isaiah Chapter 8 continues the theme already begun in Chapter 7. *Immanuel* is mentioned again in the sense that He is the true representative of the nation. Assyria is considered an ally by Ahaz, King of Judah; but considered an enemy by Isaiah. In fact, Isaiah has committed treason in the eyes of the leadership of Judah.

Verse 1 begins with the Lord's command to Isaiah to take *"a large tablet and write on it in ordinary letters: Swift is the booty, speedy is the prey."* *Swift is the booty, speedy is the prey* means that whatever is going to happen is going to happen quickly. Think of a lion ready to spring on its prey and carry it away! The verse begins with a direction to make a huge poster: "Use bold type! Use capital letters!" (Leupold, p. 167). I remember substitute teaching for a middle school class; and, because I was so tired of the students repeatedly asking, "What page??!!," that I simply wrote out the page number so large that it covered the whole board! In a similar way, the Lord wanted Judah's attention.

The second verse continues that Isaiah was to take two "faithful" witnesses to testify before Ahaz. "Both are called 'faithful men' or witnesses because they would not have sided with the prophet against the king" (Leupold p. 167). These two men were Uriah the priest and Ahaz's father-in-law, Zechariah. These men were not faithful at all to the Lord, but were faithful instead to Ahaz. Uriah, for example, cooperated with Ahaz to construct a replica of an Assyrian altar in Jerusalem. On this altar sacrifices were made to encourage success for the approaching Assyrian king (2 Kings 16:10–16). These two witnesses were to see the especially clear and bold message Isaiah was given from the Lord (Leupold, p. 167).

Then in verse 3, we read that Isaiah had relations with his wife, "the prophetess," and she gave birth to a second son. Isaiah's wife was given the title "prophetess" because she was married to the prophet. "There is not an indication that she expressed any prophetic function" (Leupold, p. 168). In our culture, it would be akin to calling the president's wife "the First Lady." The newborn was named *"Maher-shalal-hash-baz,"* which means, "Swift is the booty, speedy is the prey," as referenced in verse 1. How interesting it is to see the comparison of Isaiah's son *Maher-shalal-hash-baz* with the mysterious child *"Immanuel"* referred to in Chapter 7. Isaiah's son was given prominence, to be sure, but hardly the prominence given to *Immanuel* (Leupold, p. 168).

Verse 4 continues with the message that before the newborn boy knows how to cry out *"Abba"* or *"Ima,"* "father" or "mother," the material substance of both Syria and Israel will be carried off by the conquering Assyrian army.

Do you think Ahaz got the message? What a relief for Judah to believe that the immediate threat of Syria and Israel would be wiped out by the Assyrian army; but were they aware that Assyria would not stop at Judah's borders?

### Expect the Unexpected (Isaiah 8:5-8, 10)

1/17/08

Verses 5-8 describe the Assyrian invasion:

*⁵ And again the LORD spoke to me further, saying,*

> *⁶ "Inasmuch as these people have rejected the gently flowing waters of Shiloah, and rejoice in Rezin and the son of Remaliah;*
>
> *⁷ "Now therefore, behold, the Lord is about to bring on them the strong and abundant waters of the Euphrates, even the king of Assyria and all his glory; and it will rise up over all its channels and go over all its banks.*
>
> *⁸ "Then it will sweep on into Judah, it will overflow and pass through, it will reach even to the neck; and the spread of its wings will fill the breadth of your land, O Immanuel."*

I am sure that Judah did not realize that Assyria would be compared to a river overflowing with flood waters, too powerful to stop or slow down. Isaiah could see it coming, but the people of Judah couldn't.

In Chapter 7, verse 14, we saw that the name of this mysterious child was *Immanuel*, "God with us." Notice that the name *Immanuel* is also mentioned here in verse 8: *"The spread of its wings will fill the breadth of your land, O Immanuel,"* referring to the swift advance of the

Assyrian army into Immanuel's land. The term is also mentioned in verse 10: *"For God is with us."*

So the question remains, whose land is it? Ultimately, it is God's. So the question is again raised, is this mysterious child *Immanuel* of Chapter 7 being compared to the Lord?

### *Is It Treason to Tell the Truth? (Isaiah 8:11-15)*

2/13/08

On another front, verses 11 and 12 are an exhortation to Isaiah not to be miffed or troubled by the accusation that he is a conspirator against the government or is committing treason. The party line was that anyone who disagreed with the policy that Assyria was to come to Judah's aid against her enemies Israel and Syria, was part of the "conspiracy" (Leupold, p. 172).

It's funny how things can be twisted in our world. Verse 12 suggests that what was actually "treasonable" was to go against the message that Isaiah was bringing. Verse 13 continues, *"It is the LORD of hosts whom you should regard as holy. And He shall be your fear, and He shall be your dread."* In verse 14 the message continues with a twist, *"Then He shall become a sanctuary."*

I am reminded of a song we used to sing in the early 70s. I was, at that time, living in New Jersey and touring with a musical group called *Messiah's Shofar*. It was Mitch, Emily, Louie, and I singing in churches. When people would ask how our group was doing we would say, "Just fine, sho far." Anyway, the song was based on a passage in Habakkuk. The prophet's faith was paramount in the midst of terrible circumstances. Yet, Habakkuk was able to exult in His Lord:

> *Though the fig tree should not blossom,*
> *And there be no fruit on the vines,*
> *Though the yield of the olive should fail,*
> *And the fields produce no food,*
> *Though the flock should be cut off from the fold,*
> *And there be no cattle in the stalls,*
> *Yet I will exult in the LORD,*
> *I will rejoice in the God of my salvation.*
> – Habakkuk 3:17-18

To be honest, the song really terrified me. Being a young believer, I was especially conscious of the tremendous power and dread of the Lord; but I was not well versed in His tremendous love and overcoming grace. So, all seemed bleak and hopeless to me. Judgment was coming, and I did not want to experience it. My choice, however, was to remain faithful with the determined belief that I would eventually understand God's love for me. I chose to believe that God would supernaturally provide a place of peace and sanctuary in the midst of trial. In my own strength I would live in fear and panic; but with His divine intervention, I could have great peace.

So, the people of Judah had a choice. It was a time of decision. They could run to the Lord for refuge, or they could choose not to do so, and the Lord would become to them as a *"stone to strike and a rock to stumble over. And many will stumble over them, then they will fall and be broken; they will even be snared and caught"* (verses 14b-15). It's safe to say we still have a choice today. We have tremendous opportunities to experience God's love and compassion in the midst of hard times, or we can try to get along in our own strength. More next time!

### Some Will Understand (Isaiah 8:16-22)

2/26/08

I don't know if you've realized it, but the section we are in is called *The Book of Immanuel* (Fruchtenbaum, cassette 3, side two). It goes from Chapter 7 through Chapter 12. In this final segment of Chapter 8, we see the utter darkness in which Israel and Judah find themselves. But the good news is that the darkness will be infused with *a great light* as described at the beginning of Chapter 9, in verse 2.

Isaiah was told by the Lord to stop writing for a while – maybe a year, maybe more (Leupold, p. 174). Verse 16 of Chapter 8 reads, *Bind up the testimony, seal the law among my disciples.* Verse 17 continues, *And I will wait for the LORD who is hiding His face from the house of Jacob; I will even look eagerly for Him.* So the principle here is that sometimes the Lord chooses to stop talking to those who do not believe; but at the same time, He still is reaching out to His own, the "remnant." Isaiah's activity was limited, as Leupold put it, "to the very small circle of the receptive ones" (p. 175).

Isn't this the same pattern *Yeshua* (Jesus) demonstrated to His disciples? It came to a point in Jesus' ministry when He chose to no longer talk to the crowds in a direct way, but instead used parables. The parables were spoken in such a way that only those who were sensitive to His way could understand them.

The good news is that there is always hope for the believer. Isaiah mentioned that he *will even look eagerly for Him* (verse 17b). "No matter how many others there are who reject God's message, His faithful followers can do nothing less than hope in Him. Hope is the banner of the faithful" (Leupold, p.175). The good news is also that hope is God given. We cannot generate it.

As I mentioned in earlier studies, at one time a great fear came over me. I had no strength to understand or deal with it. To make matters worse, my mother would look at me and say, almost as a rebuke, "Where is your faith?!" It wasn't there. She was right. I couldn't summon it on my own. In time though, the Lord was able to minister to my fear and provide for me the courage I needed.

In verse 18, Isaiah wrote: *Behold, I and the children whom the LORD has given me are for signs and wonders in Israel.* He felt he and his family were being used by God to be an example for Israel. In essence, he was saying, "Look at me and my children!" (Leupold, p. 175). Whoa. Wait a minute. Isn't that a bit much to claim for yourself and your kids, Isaiah? The Apostle Paul (Saul) exhorted his disciples to use him (Paul) as an example. *The things you have learned and received and heard and seen in me, practice these things; and the God of peace shall be with you* (Philippians 4:9). However, Paul wasn't as bold as to say his example was for "signs and wonders in Israel."

Verses 19 through 22 show the depth of Judah and Israel's downfall. For their refuge and security, they put their trust in mediums and spiritists who *whisper and mutter* (verse 19). As Leupold put it, in this case: "The man who sees is seeking, as a guide, the man who is blind" (p. 177).

So they have descended into deep darkness, but the wonderful contrast is that Chapter 9 will show how *a great light* will infiltrate the land. More next time.

# Isaiah Chapter 9 "And His Name Will Be Called"

3/09/08

"I have just read Chapter 9." ___ yes

*Out of Darkness into Light (Isaiah 9:1)*

A trip on the Long Island Railroad to New York City from the simple town of Merrick can be a big adventure for a child. You pass many smaller villages; and, as you peer through the windows, you can sense the personality of each little train station. Except, when you enter Queens, things abruptly change. The quaint little towns transform into multitudes of high-rise apartment complexes and large train yards. In the distance you can get glimpses of the New York City skyline. When you are about to leave the Island, you can sense the train descending lower and lower until you suddenly find yourself engulfed in the darkness. You're in a tunnel rumbling under the East River. All you can see are a few dim lights here and there. I had often wondered what would happen if the tunnel caved in and water rushed in from the East River above us while we were in the train. It would make a good movie.

Well, the story always had a happy ending, because we would eventually reach Penn Station, exit the train, walk up the steps, look for signs to the city streets, and eventually find ourselves in the wonderful light of this bustling, exciting city.

Of course on a grander scale, Israel and Judah found themselves in deep darkness at this juncture. The JPS *Tanakh:* The Holy Scriptures translation (Army edition), describes it as *"outspread thick darkness."* The English language Alexander Harkavy Bible translation of the Old Testament reads, *"trouble and darkness, dimness of anguish."* So, the end of Chapter 8 did not leave much hope.

To give a little history, according to Leupold, "The date may well be shortly after Tiglath-Pileser's invasion of Syria and Ephraim (Israel) from 734 to 732 BCE. That would account for the desolate state of the upper Galilee ..." which was mentioned at the beginning of Chapter 9 (p. 180).

Galilee mentioned in Chapter 9?! What about Galilee? *Yeshua* taught extensively in Galilee.

Chapter 9, verse 1, reads, *But there will be no more gloom for her who was in anguish; in earlier times He treated the land of Zebulun and the land of Naphtali with contempt, but later on He shall make it glorious, by the way of the sea, on the other side of Jordan, Galilee of the Gentiles.*

Sometimes the Jewish translations and Christian translations of the *Tanakh* (Old Testament) have different ordering systems for chapter and verse. The Jewish translations place Chapter 9, verse 1 as the last verse of Chapter 8. Thus, the New American Standard Bible's 9:1, for example, is 8:23 in the JPS *Tanakh:* The Holy Scriptures. So we now have a problem. When the Jewish translations make 9:1 to be the last verse of Chapter 8, they are teaching that the affliction on the Galilee region is a product of the Assyrian invasion. For example, the Harkavy translation reads:

*... for he is not weary that oppresseth her: in the former time he lightly afflicted the land of Zebulun and the land of Naphtali, and in the latter time **he did more grievously afflict her** by the way of the sea, beyond Jordan, in Galilee of the nations.*

The JPS *Tanakh:* The Holy Scripture (U.S. Army edition) reads:

*...the former [king] hath lightly afflicted the land of Zebulun and the land of Naphtali – but the latter **hath dealt a more grievous blow** by the way of the sea, beyond the Jordan, in the district of the nations.*

The *Tanakh:* The Holy Scriptures reads:

*Only the former king would have brought abasement to the land of Zebulun and the land of Nephthali – while the latter one **would have brought honor** to the Way of the Sea, the other side of the Jordan and Galilee of the Nations.*

Compare these translations with the New American Standard Bible (NASB), which reads:

*But there will be no more gloom for her who was in anguish; in earlier times, He treated the land of Zebulun and the land of Nephthali with contempt, but later on He **shall make it glorious**, by the way of the sea, on the other side of Jordan, Galilee of the Gentiles.*

The NASB indicates that the Messiah is the one who is working in this passage, at first in a heavy way and then in a glorious way.

More next time!

### Three Points of View (Isaiah 9:1-2)

3/21/08

In the memorable musical *Fiddler on the Roof,* the main character Tevye finds himself in the midst of a discussion between two rabbinical students. One held a certain position and the other held the opposite view. As Tevye heard the first argument, he said to that individual, "You are right." After hearing the second argument, he said to the other individual, "You are right." An observer pointed out the discrepancy and said to Tevye, "You can't say *he* is right and then say *he* is right!" To which Tevye responded, "You are right!" It has been mused that when you get two Jewish people together, you get three opinions.

In our last study it was mentioned that there was a difference between the Jewish translations of Isaiah 8:23 and the Christian translations of 9:1. I have found that they are similar in one way. We find that the word in question in Hebrew is *hikabid*. Hebrew is neat because studying it is like figuring out a puzzle, and you have to be sort of a detective. You can find smaller words hidden within bigger words. In the midst of the word *hikabid* is the root word *kbd* or *kavod*. The word essentially means "glorious" but also means "a weight, heaviness and a sense of honor" (Brown, Driver, and Briggs, p. 457).

In every Jewish synagogue throughout the world, the revered *Shema* is recited every week. It proclaims: "Hear O Israel, the Lord is our God, the Lord is one" or in Hebrew: *"Shema Yisrael Adonai Elohenu Adonai echad."* In the second verse of the *Shema* we can find the word *kavod*: *"Baruch shem **kavod** malchuto l'olam va'ed"* which in English is "Blessed is His name whose **glorious** kingdom is forever and ever." We can also find the word in Chapter 6 of Isaiah, verse 3, when the *seraphim* are proclaiming, *"Holy, Holy, Holy, is the LORD of hosts. The whole earth is full of His **glory**."* So both Jewish and Christian translators agree that the word *glory* is a heavy one, demanding honor, and can easily afflict and deal a grievous blow to those in its presence. Heavy stuff.

We need to talk a little about the area in verse 1 affected by the "great light" (9:2). It was the tribal territory of Zebulon that lay directly west of the Sea of Galilee. Also mentioned is Naphtali that extended farther north and pushed down between the sea and Zebulon. The mentioned "sea road" was a passage along the west side of the sea. In addition, the "land beyond the Jordan" is the area east of the Sea of Galilee. The term "Galilee of the Nations" refers chiefly to north Galilee (Leupold, pp. 181-2).

As for the word "Galilee," no one seems to know where the name came from. Some have suggested it means "a circle." In modern times, Christian tours to Israel know the name of the lake to be "The Sea of Galilee," but Israelis know the lake to be the *"Kinneret,"* meaning, "the harp" because this body of water is shaped as such.

So the question still remains, what is the *great light* of verse 2 that will be affecting this area? Is it indeed the Messiah who will appear some 750 years later, or is the *great light* more of a symbolic entity indicating that in the future time the area will recover from the devastating Assyrian invasion? We'll explore this more next time.

## The Key of Promise (Isaiah 9:1, 2)

5/08/08

It was discussed last time that there was a discrepancy between the Jewish translations of Isaiah 8:23, and the Christian translations of Isaiah 9:1. Upon further study, I found a lot of Christian translations that read the text in the same way as the Jewish translations do. They emphasize that the manifested "glory" affecting the land of Zebulon and Naphtali is a heavy one, creating honor and awe, and one that can have a grievous effect. For example, compare Isaiah 9:1 in the following Bible versions:

The New International Version:

> ... *in the future he will honor Galilee of the Gentiles, by the way of the sea, along the Jordan ...*

The King James Version:

> ... *and afterward did more grievously afflict her by the way of the sea, beyond Jordan, in Galilee of the nations ...*

The Darby Edition:

> ... *afterwards heavily, visited the land of Zebulon and the land of Naphtali, – the way of the sea, beyond the Jordan ...*

When thinking of those walking in darkness having seen a great light (verse 2), I am reminded of a particular scene in the classic work by John Bunyan, *The Pilgrim's Progress*. Christian was kept in Doubting Castle as a prisoner. He was in a dungeon. He was too discouraged to attempt any escape. Finally, upon resorting to a meager prayer, he realized that he had something in his heart. He reached inside, and in his heart he found "the key of promise." He took the key out, and with it he was able to unlock the door to his cell. Then he found that the same key was able to open the castle door. He had gained his freedom from Doubting Castle by utilizing a mustard seed of faith. It really takes a little step of faith on our part to see the magnificent and mighty works of God on our behalf. A friend of mine told me today that he cannot tell anyone how big God is because whatever he describes as big will still be very small compared to God.

When I was in seminary in the early 1970s, I was in my own "Doubting Castle." I couldn't study, I couldn't think, and I was afraid all the time. I was afraid the world, as I knew it, was going to end very soon. The faculty at the school asked me to go to the counseling center and take a Meyers Briggs Psychology Analysis Test. How humiliating! You can't pass or fail the test, but I failed it anyway! My best friend, at that time, was also asked to do the same and he wouldn't. He chickened out. He went on to have a very successful ministry. But I was the crazy one. Of course I was praying for answers and relief.

Corrie ten Boom, a famous Christian, Holocaust survivor, and author of *The Hiding Place,* was speaking at the Biola Chapel in Southern California at that time; and I lived close by that college and decided to attend. After her talk I asked if I could speak with Corrie, and she agreed to see me. She listened to my story and said, "Do you think you are the only one?" Powerful words. I had not considered the fact that many others were going through the same experiences I was, and that encouraged me. I was able to pray with Corrie ten Boom, and felt a tremendous dose of God's compassion. It was the beginning of my journey out of "Doubting Castle." I had seen a great light.

### *Have Seen, Will See (Isaiah 9:2)*

*5/15/08*

Can we continue with this same passage, or are we beating a dead horse? It will take years to complete this book! I take comfort in the thought that at least we will complete it before I die because within those chapters is a wealth of spiritual food to chew on and enough for those seeking the Lord to find Him.

So, since you haven't responded in a negative way, I am going to proceed with this quite large and challenging task. I must say that the more I venture into this study, the more I am humbled and at the same time amazed at how deep the written Word is.

I guess we've completed our study of verse 1, so let's continue with Isaiah 9:2. I was reading an ESL (English as a Second Language) method book the other day. The author recommended that grammar be taught only after the student reads something or hears something. Then you can use what was read or heard to teach the grammar point. Grammar should not be taught the other way around. So, the Harkavy, KJV, NIV, and Darby translations, for example, say, *The people who walk in darkness* **have seen** *a great light,* and the NASB reads, *The people who walk in darkness* **will see** *a great light.* Why the difference?

For you linguists and grammarians, Dr. David L. Cooper in his work, *Messiah: His Nature and Person* (p. 186), explains it this way:

> The reader's attention has been called to the fact that the "time element" does not appear in the Hebrew verb as in ancient Greek, modern English, German, and other languages. The so-called perfect tense of the Hebrew verb simply expresses completed action, which according to the

drift of the thought, may be translated as past perfect, present perfect, or future perfect. [For example, something was done, is being done, or will be done.] The context in each case is to determine the choice of the proper tense in English to convey the exact meaning of the verb in its original setting.

For those of you who hated grammar in school, and would rather not think about it, but would rather be listening to some good jazz, or sunning on the beach, or hiking somewhere, I feel great sympathy; but please hang in here with me for a couple of minutes. The Hebrew has a form called the "prophetic perfect" where the future is explained as having already occurred. This concept may sound weird, like something out of the *Twilight Zone* or from a *Far Side* cartoon panel, but it is also quite an interesting concept, as we shall see.

So the Harkavy, KJV, NIV, and Darby translations are technically more accurate than the NASB translation, using *the people who walk in darkness **have seen** a great light* to indicate that this revelation of light is sure to occur in the future, just as sure as if it had already happened. However, the NASB expresses the passage in a way that we English speakers can better understand it by saying, *the people who walk in darkness **will see** a great light.*

But what if we could use the prophetic perfect in English? It would be nice to say that the house has been paid in full, or the visa balance has been paid off. We could write it, or proclaim it; and, sometime in the future, the statement would come to pass! We wouldn't want to parallel the "name it, claim it" folks who border on telling God what is and is not to be. We can't presume upon God. We cannot generate or muster up a faith. Our faith needs to be God given. The prophetic perfect kind of faith doesn't work unless God is inspiring the thought, and we are resting in His confidence.

I remember a preacher once testifying that he believed so strongly in God's intervention in a certain area that he could reach out his hand and "touch it." He saw it as if it were already there. His belief is a graphic illustration of one's faith when inspired by the Lord.

We can offer a mustard seed of faith, and we can pray, "Lord, I believe. Help me with my unbelief." And when we do, our Lord may take that small step and increase our faith to believe in such a way that in our minds it has already happened.

More next time.

### *Rejoicing and Restoration (Isaiah 9:3-5, 6)*
6/19/08

Chapter 9, verse 3, tells of rejoicing! We rejoice when we lose a few pounds, or break a bad habit or two, and then start a good habit. We're happy when we get a new house, car, computer, or boat. We rejoice at those occasions when our kids or we, ourselves, graduate from some fine institution. Engagements, weddings, birthdays, baby showers, anniversaries, bar and bat mitzvahs, and confirmations invoke our joy. We also rejoice when someone finds our Lord and enters into the new life He offers.

There is tremendous rejoicing in verses 3-5 because of deliverance, deliverance from the oppression of the Assyrians. The evidence of the deliverance is the fact that He will "multiply the nation" (Leupold, p. 183).

Bugs Bunny received a phone call, and the caller told Bugs, "If you can answer this one question, you can win $10,000 dollars!" (I don't really remember the amount or the details of this cartoon, but I'll give you the gist of it.) Well, Bugs Bunny gave his consent; and the announcer said, "Mr. Bunny, what is 1,052 times 648?" Bugs said, "Aw, that's easy. It's 681,696." "That's right, Mr. Bunny!" replied the caller, "You win the $10,000 dollars! By the way, Mr. Bunny, how did you come up with the answer so quickly?" "Well," Bugs explained, "If there's anything us bunnies can do, it's multiply."

So, in other words, the population of Israel and Judah will be restored. As Leupold explains that "… after the Assyrians were done with their ravaging, it [the Galilee] will again be populous and thriving … [in] the Messianic days …. In Jesus' time, as also Josephus reports, Galilee was dotted with numerous prosperous villages" (p. 183). Josephus was a Jewish historian who lived in the first century.

Apparently, as the nation is multiplied physically, their "gladness" will also increase; maybe even multiply.

Judah and Israel will be glad being in the Lord's presence, and even though we may have a hard time relating to it, being modern city folk, their rejoicing will be similar to that of taking in a great harvest, or winning a tremendous battle.

Gideon's victory over Midian is mentioned in verse 4. Apparently it was a battle foremost in the Jewish mind of that day, because, as you can remember, Gideon went to war with only 300 men, and it was the Lord who delivered the Midianites into Gideon's hand (Judges 6-8) (Leupold, p. 184). Perhaps the Assyrians will fall in the same way!

Verse 5 continues by saying that the warrior's boots and bloody cloaks will be burned in the fire. Such is an indication that the fighting has ceased, and that war is truly over. It's an anticipation of a time when peace will reign for Israel and Judah (Leupold, p. 184).

Interestingly enough, this kind of rejoicing segues into one of the most powerful Messianic passages of the Hebrew Scriptures, Chapter 9, verse 6.

> *For a child will be born to us, a son will be given to us;*
> *And the government will rest on His shoulders;*
> *And His name will be called,*
> *Wonderful Counselor, Mighty God,*
> *Eternal Father, Prince of Peace.*

We'll begin exploring these powerful names next time!

### What Is His Name? (Isaiah 9:6)
7/06/08

*For a child will be born to us, a son will be given to us.* Here in Isaiah 9:6, we see the second mention of this mysterious child. As mentioned before, the first mention of the child was found in Isaiah 7:14, *"Behold, a virgin will be with child and bear a son, and she will call His name Immanuel* [God with us]." The Chapter 9 passage gives us much more detail.

Verse 9:6 continues with the phrase, *and the government will rest upon His shoulders.* The responsibility of the whole nation will be laid upon this child's shoulders. We have heard various expressions such as, "Put your head on my shoulder," "Shoulder the burden," and "The responsibility will be placed upon your shoulders." We also have the imagery of the shepherd carrying his sheep on his shoulders.

The King's name will be called, *"Wonderful Counselor," "Mighty God," "Eternal Father,"* and *"Prince of Peace."*

Fruchtenbaum (cassette 3, side two) says that, in Hebrew, the term *wonderful* here, describing the child's name, is a term only applied to God. Such is a bold statement because in Jewish thinking, God cannot be born to earth as a Child or a Son. God would forever be in heaven. Such thinking would be blasphemy and idol worship.

For many years I have struggled with the claim that the appearance of *the angel of the LORD* in Scripture was actually the appearance of God. I had always assumed that the angel was a messenger of the Lord, so much in character with the Lord that people talked to him as if talking to the Lord. However, now I have been challenged to see if what Fruchtenbaum claims about the adjective *wonderful* (cassette 3, side two) is true as it relates to God. In the following passage, we can see that the *angel of the LORD* is indeed God, and the adjective *wonderful* describes His name. Let's look at that together.

In Judges Chapter 13 we read the account of how *the angel of the LORD* visited the parents of Samson in order to announce and to prepare them for Samson's birth. After an initial appearance and then a second, Manoah and his wife engaged in a conversation with the angel about the fact that Samson would be a Nazarite, would not be able to cut his hair, and would begin to deliver Israel from the hands of the oppressive Philistines. He would be a *"Nazarite to God from the womb to the day of his death"* (verse 7). They did not know that they were talking to *the angel of the LORD*. Finally Manoah asked *the angel of the LORD, "What is your name, so that when your words come to pass, we may honor you?"* (verse 17). The angel replied, *"Why do you ask my name, seeing it is wonderful?"* (verse 18).

After a subsequent burnt offering, *when the flame went up from the altar toward heaven, the angel of the LORD ascended in the flame of the altar. When Manoah and his wife saw this, they fell on their faces to the ground* (verse 20). The passage continues, *Then Manoah knew that he was the angel of the LORD* (verse 21). *So Manoah said to his wife, "We shall surely die, for we have seen God"* (verse 22).

So, here is a powerful example of how the adjective *wonderful* is employed to describe God. There are more examples as well.

### Wonderful! (Isaiah 9:6)

7/29/08

So, for the most part, it's true! The word for *wonderful* in Isaiah 9:6 does refer to God or to some characteristic of God. There are a couple of passages though that can, but do not necessarily, refer to a quality of God. (Maybe yes, maybe no.) According to *Young's Analytical Concordance of the Bible* (p. 1067), the base word for *wonderful* in Hebrew is *p-l-a*, the Hebrew letters *peh, lamed, and aleph*, respectively. In Hebrew, though, we read from right to left, backwards so to speak, so the letters actually are read from right to left as *aleph-lamed-peh* starting with the *peh* (*p*) which is then *a-l-p*. That's just to keep you honest and heading in the right direction!

Depending on which vowels are inserted between the base letters *a-l-p*, the use of the word changes a little, but it still means "wonderful." We can see the same pattern in English in the base word *s-ng*. The application changes a bit according to which vowel you insert between the *s* and the *ng*, but the meaning remains the same. So we can read "sing," "sang," or "sung." Similarly we can insert letters in the *r-ng* format to come up with "ring," "rang," or "rung." (Anyone for "bring, brang, brung"? Just kidding. English doesn't really work the same way that Hebrew does when it comes to base words.)

The following is a list of some of the verses using the word *p-l-a*, or, *wonderful*, in different ways. See if you agree that the word does refer to God or to an attribute of God.

In the first five references (in Samuel, Proverbs, Job, and Psalms), the base word means "to be or become wonderful":

**2 Samuel 1:26b** – *"Your love to me was more **wonderful** than the love of women."*

In this passage, David is mourning over the death of Jonathan, King Saul's son. Jonathan's love for David was greater than the love of women, so maybe it is referring to the wonderful love of God. (Maybe yes, maybe no. What do you think?)

**Proverbs 30:18** – *There are three things which are too **wonderful** for me, four which I do not understand.*

Solomon is describing the way of an eagle in the sky, a serpent on a rock, a ship in the middle of the sea, and the way of a man with a maid. Is Solomon mentioning an attribute of God in the way He creates? (Maybe yes, maybe no. What is your opinion?)

**Job 42:3** – *"Therefore I have declared that which I did not understand, things too **wonderful** for me, things which I did not know."*

Job is here confessing that the things of God are too wonderful. He is repenting before God.

**Psalm 40:5** – *Many, O LORD my God, are the **wonders**, which Thou hast done.*

**Psalm 111:4** – *He has made His **wonders** to be remembered; the LORD is gracious and compassionate.*

The next two references to the root word for *wonderful* mean "to make wonderful." Do you think these reflect characteristics of God?

**2 Chronicles 2:9b** – *"... for the house which I am about to build will be great and **wonderful**."*

King Solomon is here describing the Temple that he is planning to build for the Lord. (Do you think these apply to God's character? Maybe yes, maybe no.)

**Isaiah 28:29** – *This also comes from the LORD of hosts, Who has made His counsel **wonderful** and His wisdom great.*

The next reference to the root word for *wonderful* means "to be or become wonderful."

**Psalm 139:14a** – *I will give thanks to Thee, for I am fearfully and **wonderfully** made ....*

The final three references to the root word for *wonderful* that we are considering mean "anything wonderful." Do you see any connection that applies to God in these verses?

**Psalm 119:129** – *Thy testimonies are **wonderful** ....*

**Isaiah 25:1** – *O lord, Thou art my God; I will exalt Thee, I will give thanks to Thy name; for Thou hast worked **wonders**, plans formed long ago with perfect faithfulness.*

**Isaiah 9:6** – *For a child will be born to us, a son will be given to us; and the government will rest on His shoulders; and His name will be called **Wonderful** Counselor, Mighty God, Eternal Father, Prince of Peace.*

So here we are back to Isaiah 9:6. Quite profound to see that in this mysterious child's name is the word *wonderful*, an adjective ascribed to God Almighty. We have more aspects of His name to explore, so we'll begin with *Counselor* next time!

### More than a Counselor (Isaiah 9:6)

9/14/08

Last time we explored the concept that the word *Wonderful* in Isaiah 9:6 refers mostly to a quality of God. The word following *Wonderful* in Isaiah 9:6 is *Counselor*. The Hebrew meaning for the word *counselor* is not what we in Western society think of when we think of a counselor. We think of a "shrink." For our international readers, a shrink, according to the *American Heritage College Dictionary*, is slang for "psychotherapist." I recently introduced a friend of mine, whom I have known for 30 years, as my "old shrink." I don't think he appreciated it. He just wanted to be known as a good friend. But it's true! After I dropped out of seminary in 1977, I embarked on 18 months of individual counseling and 5 years of group counseling with my shrink as the group leader. As a result, I know a lot about counseling and the family dynamics that go along with it. I'm an amateur expert!

But the word *Counselor* here in verse 6 is more a term describing how one performs in political office. Leupold writes that this child "will be most effective in planning, in formulating a plan for action. A great work is to be done by Him, even the greatest ever attempted .... In fact, the very plan, as such, is a marvel: therefore a marvel of a counselor" (p. 185).

Some translations place a comma between *Wonderful* and *Counselor*, making them two separate names. It appears as *Wonderful, Counselor*. Other translations use *Wonderful* as an adjective describing Counselor; and, thus, no comma is used between the words. This rendering, *Wonderful Counselor,* is better because it follows the pattern shown in the following couplets: *Mighty God, Eternal Father,* and *Prince of Peace.*

Jewish Translations have a different twist when looking at the four couplets of Isaiah 9:6. The Alexander Harkavy translation reads, *And His name will be called Wonderful, Counselor of the Mighty God, of the Everlasting Father, Prince of Peace.* In essence, their translation says that the child will be a counselor *of* God, but not God. This translation is really based on presupposition. However, the Hebrew here is a lot simpler than that, and doesn't have the word *of* in it until it says, *Prince of Peace.*

The Jewish Publication Society (U.S. Army edition) reads, *And his name is called Pele-joez-el-gibbor-abi-ad-sar-shalom.* That's an imaginative way to deal with the problem! They just listed the words in Hebrew! How many read or understand Hebrew? To their credit, they do place a footnote at the bottom of the page giving an honest translation:

"That is, Wonderful in counsel is God the Mighty, the everlasting Father, the Ruler of Peace."

The JPS *Tanakh: The Holy Scripture* version takes great liberty in translating the passage. It reads: *For a child has been born to us, a son has been given us. And authority has settled on his shoulders. He has been named "The Mighty God is planning grace; The Eternal Father, a peaceable ruler" – in token of abundant authority and of peace without limit ...*

It is good to know that this mysterious child is called "Counselor" because we need to know that the Almighty One has planned and formulated a good plan for our world and also our lives.

### All Powerful for the Good (Isaiah 9:6)

10/10/08

*El Gibbor* means "All Mighty, All Powerful God." As was mentioned earlier, Isaiah 9:6 has four couplets for the name of this mysterious child who will become "ruler" in Israel. They are the following, "Wonderful Counselor, Mighty God, Everlasting Father, and Prince of Peace."

Leupold comments on the name *Mighty God as* follows: "The individual in question possesses the capacity for carrying out to the full, all that His brilliant plans call for. He has nothing less than the full omnipotence of God at His command. What He devised, He is also well able to achieve. He is Himself God" (pp. 185-186).

When we think of one who is all powerful, the position can be good or it can be bad. One can have ultimate power and be brutal. This powerful individual could be motivated by fear and the need to control. Many a dictator has come and gone with this oppressive quality.

Nevertheless, in Isaiah 9:6 we see that this mysterious child will be all powerful and yet also have a nature that will enable Him to use His power for the good instead of evil. His power is accompanied by His ability to govern and make decisions for the benefit of mankind. His power is embedded in the qualities of a benevolent Father who will always be with us, and His motive will be peace.

A respected family member once said that the only hope for this world is "a dictator who loves the people." He will be one who has ultimate power but will use his power to benefit his people. In a way he was right because when the Messiah comes, His Kingdom will not be a Republic or a Democracy, but a Theocracy. He will rule the earth with love, compassion, justice, and fairness. (You can read more about this in Isaiah Chapter 11.)

On the other hand, when the "false messiah" or "antichrist" comes, he will mask himself as the hope for mankind. He will be dynamic, popular, compassionate, assertive, and will present himself as wanting the best for mankind. He will solve the economic and political problems of our day and will come to power because the world will be desperate for a sound, trustworthy leader who can take us out of this mess. He will unite our world religiously, politically, and economically. He will make a pact with Israel to secure peace for her and her neighbors. He will make Jerusalem an international city, rebuild the Temple, and will solve the Israeli/Palestinian problem. He will require everyone to sign up for his economic plan by taking an identification mark in order to buy and sell things. His policies will work for those who buy into his plan. But please don't be fooled. Those who refuse to take his mark will have to go into hiding. He will eventually show his true colors. He will turn against Israel and will persecute all who will not turn and worship him. He will thrust our world into the ultimate holocaust. The Scriptures caution us to be skeptical of those who say, "Peace, peace when there is no peace." In Jeremiah 6:14, it says: *"And they have healed the brokenness of My people superficially, saying, 'Peace, peace,' but there is no peace."*

The Child in Isaiah 9:6 is the true Messiah. Come and find Him. For those who have already found Him, abide in His love and comfort. Rest in the fact that He is the Mighty God and is All Powerful.

## **Father Forever (Isaiah 9:6-7)**
11/2/08

The following is what Leupold says about Isaiah 9, verses 6 and 7. "It goes without saying that this is one of the clearest and most meaningful Messianic prophesies in the whole Old Testament" (p. 187).

Just as a refresher, verses 6-7 say:

> *⁶ For a child will be born to us, a son will be given to us; and the government will rest on His shoulders; and His name will be called Wonderful Counselor, Mighty God, Eternal Father, Prince of Peace. ⁷ There will be no end to the increase of His government or of peace, on the throne of David and over His kingdom, to establish it and to uphold it with justice and righteousness from then on and forevermore. The zeal of the LORD of hosts will accomplish this.*

We have already discussed the first and second of these four couplets, *Wonderful Counselor* and *Mighty God.* It seems that the commentators I have looked at do not have much to add to what is already plainly seen here.

So let's take a look at the third couplet, *Eternal Father*. Some translations list it as *Father of Eternity* or *Everlasting Father*. Leupold makes it easier: *"Father Forever"* (p. 186). In other words, the emphasis is not on the individual's eternal existence, but that of his being everlastingly a Father. The child will have the qualities of a father, "having loving, paternal concern for those who have been committed to His charge" (p. 186). But Leupold is emphatic in saying that there is not even a remote reference here to an "inter-Trinitarian relationship – the Son being called the Father. It is better to simply compare Him to a father, i.e.: a father has compassion, so the LORD does as well" (p. 186).

For those of us who did not have an assertive earthly father, this concept of "Father Forever" will be difficult to grasp. Rocky Fleming wrote for Influencers, an effective men's ministry, and said it this way:

> Most believers believe that God knows us thoroughly and He cares for us, but we really do not believe He is willing to come to our help. We believe it for someone else. We believe it when someone shares their own story. Yet when it comes down to us, we become doubting Thomases. [*The American Heritage Dictionary* says that a doubting Thomas is one who is habitually doubtful.] Thomas, the disciple, did not believe that Jesus had risen from death until he could see proof. For this reason many of the trials we face become ours to carry rather than our accepting God's help. He wants to prove Himself to us. He is in fact saying, "Trust Me to

get you through this; and in doing so I will prove Myself to you and, thus, draw you closer to Me."

There is very little comfort if we have a God who is involved with us on a deep level we've been speaking of but is unable to do anything about it. There is great comfort to know that the Great I Am, the Creator of the universe, is my *Abba*, my Daddy; and He is able to do something about what He knows and cares about. Knowing this brings us great comfort when we face those impossible situations that only He can remedy. We need to know this aspect of God to draw closer to Him. (*The Journey Participant Manual*, p. 14)

So we begin to realize the meaning of *Father Forever* as not just a title, but as part of a relationship offered by God to us. This mysterious child's name carries with it the powerful qualities of One who is always with us when we open up to Him and allow Him to always provide for us as an effectual, active, caring, and benevolent Father. Next time we will take a look at the fourth couplet of Isaiah 9:6: *Prince of Peace*.

### Beth Sar Shalom (Isaiah 9:6)
11/22/08

*Prince of Peace* (in Hebrew, *Sar Shalom*), is the fourth couplet listed in Isaiah 9:6b: *And His name will be called Wonderful Counselor, Mighty God, Eternal Father, Prince of Peace.*

The name *Prince of Peace* has special significance for me because, in the early 1970s, I attended a little congregation in New York

City called *Beth Sar Shalom,* which means "House of the Prince of Peace." I have many fond memories of that place.

*Beth Sar Shalom* was the active congregation of the American Board of Missions to the Jews, now called, Chosen People Ministries. The congregational leader, Charlie Eisenberg, was a recent graduate from Talbot Seminary. The tiny congregation had maybe six or seven rows of old wooden pews with an aisle running down the middle. At the front of the room was a stage, and on the stage was a big, red curtain with two large, golden lions embroidered on it. I remember that the lions were facing each other. I had always wondered what was behind that curtain – maybe Torah scrolls?

So the congregation had a Jewish name, with a Jewish congregational leader, and a Jewish curtain. But the name of the congregation refers back to our passage in Isaiah, and the congregational leader believed in *Yeshua*, Jesus; and to my surprise, behind that magnificent curtain was a baptismal!

One Saturday, I remember sitting next to the center aisle, in the right side set of pews. My friend Rich, also a new believer in *Yeshua*, was sitting next to me. We were listening to a very serious message from Rachmiel Frydland, a respected, believing rabbi and teacher who had survived the Holocaust. While we were concentrating on the message, a large cockroach passed us. It was happily prancing along the top of the pew in front of us. When our unexpected visitor reached the end of the pew, it leaped into the air, jumping for its life, down to the carpet below. This experience was so surprising and spontaneous that Rich and I could not help but start laughing uncontrollably, and we could not stop! Of course our speaker did not understand our response to his message. I think God has a sense of humor.

In time, I was also immersed, or baptized, at that congregation. When I invited my father and mother to attend the ceremony, they would not come. That was hard for me because my father always taught me to believe whatever I wanted. I was free to explore. But when I did express a faith that was in his mind offensive to the Jewish faith, he did not support me. My mother, to her credit, did defend me when relatives or friends questioned her about my newborn faith. She would say, "I think it's great that he is standing up for what he believes; and besides, all the early believers in Jesus were Jewish." In retrospect, I think it would have been better to wait and be immersed at a later time. I needed more time to understand and reflect upon my new faith.

### Clara and Joe (Isaiah 9:6)
3/22/09

*Beth Sar Shalom* also held meetings on Long Island! Clara and Joe Ruben hosted them in their home. I heard about Clara and Joe Ruben's Long Island meeting from people who attended the *Beth Sar Shalom* Congregation in New York City. When I called Clara to get information, she immediately made me feel at ease. Filled with joy and encouragement, with a few Yiddish phrases mixed in, she yelled and screamed as she gave me the details. When I asked her what time her meeting started, she replied, "Well it's supposed to start at 7:30, but nobody comes until 8:00, and the teacher doesn't get there until 8:30. So, come whenever you want!" That's called Jewish Standard Time!

When I arrived at their home, I was greeted with a big pinch on the cheek, you know, the kind that leaves a bruise for a couple of weeks because all the blood is forced out of the area where the facial skin was temporarily disfigured. (Not many people do that these days. Maybe it's considered physical abuse of some kind.) She also gave me a big hug and a kiss. She was a little lady, and her husband Joe was gentle and mild mannered.

Upon entering the first room, you could see the incredible spread of pastries, cheesecake, black & whites, cream- and fruit-filled Danishes, and coffee cakes. It was a diabetic's nightmare. I was not a diabetic at that time and freely indulged myself, shamelessly. It was then termed a Jewish heaven!

The Bible study was held in the next room. We all sat around a large table waiting for the teacher, Marty, to arrive. Marty was a young, thin, tall, energetic businessman type, with a white shirt and a tie and a thick Brooklyn accent. He seemed to me to be self-taught in the Scriptures. We all sat around a large table in the den as Marty first took prayer requests and then taught us about Messianic prophecy. I distinctly remember a prayer request for one woman's cat. Marty was obviously surprised at this request but resigned to pray for the little creature. This was unusual because, in the synagogue, whoever heard of someone praying for a cat? Anyway, his prayer was something like this, "Oh Lord, we pray for Mrs. Bronson's little puddy cat."

You could see that Clara and Joe, the leaders of this congenial group, had a deep love for each other. Years later, Clara explained that Joe was not the same after a man, sitting next to him on a park bench, was shot down in cold blood. Clara was able to report that calmly and clearly as if it was just part of life as a believer. She would often exclaim, "I have a lot of faith!" At first, I would balk at the statement as if she had false pride; but later on I began to see it as humility. One so dedicated to the Lord would not say things lightly, and her claim was actually a statement of helplessness and need as she trusted our Lord on a moment-by-moment basis.

### Hilda (Isaiah 9:6)

3/22/09

Before we get back to studying the term *Prince of Peace* in Isaiah 9:6, I want to make mention of one more worker for *Beth Sar Shalom*. Hilda Koser was in charge of the Coney Island work. She was a firebrand. She called her little mission her castle. It was spotless. She could smell dirt and was relentless in finding and eliminating it. Hilda Koser had an intense impact on the children who attended her Daily Vacation Bible Schools. Children from broken homes found the Lord there. Hilda built strong relationships with the Black community living around her mission, and everyone loved her. When the Jewish Defense League, a militant group dedicated to defending the Jewish community, came to do harm to her building, the residents in her neighborhood protected her. She taught me that complete dedication to our Lord was the ideal. She never stopped loving and encouraging. She was a pillar of the faith and has much reward in heaven.

### Dr. Feinberg (Isaiah 9:6)

4/04/09

When Hilda Koser knew that I was planning to attend Talbot Seminary the following fall, she encouraged me and also gave me a warning. The warning was that when I got to Talbot, I would experience subtle anti-Semitism. She told me the story of a Jewish believer who attended another famous seminary deemed, "the older sister of Talbot." This gentleman was so freaked out that he literally jumped out of his dormitory window and left the school! She encouraged me by saying that I reminded her of the Dean at Talbot Seminary, Charles Lee Feinberg.

Dr. Charles Feinberg was a scholar of scholars. He was studying to be a rabbi for 8 years before he found the Lord. A godly woman prayed for him three times a day for those 8 years. He received his Doctorate in Archaeology from Johns Hopkins University and his theological degrees from Dallas Seminary. He could speak eight languages fluently. He wrote most of the Old Testament notes for the *New Scofield Reference Bible*, and also authored a number of Bible commentaries. I remember how all the other professors at Talbot looked up to him. When I entered seminary, Dr. Feinberg took me under his wing. I remember praying in his office. He once told us that prayer was work. It can be a struggle.

He always had a quick joke or funny story to share in class. One exchange I remember to this day was when he asked us students to define the word *procrastinate*. I raised my hand and said, "Dr. Feinberg, it means to think very hard about something." He shook his head and said, "Noooo." Then a student named Laurence, the son of a Japanese missionary, raised his hand and said, "Dr. Feinberg, I've been meaning to look up that word, but I just haven't gotten around to it." Dr. Feinberg said, "Ah, Laurence, a man after my own heart." Dr. Feinberg then continued, "Noooo. Procrastinate means to 'put off.' The next time you're approaching Talbot Seminary on a bus, ask the driver to please 'procrastinate' you on the corner."

We will continue our study of Isaiah in the next issue. We are currently in Isaiah, Chapter 9, verse 6, discussing *Sar Shalom, the Prince of Peace.*

### Dad (Isaiah 9:6)

12/31/10

Oh, where was I now? That's right, Isaiah Chapter 9 and the topic of the *Prince of Peace.* I simply can't leave this topic until I tell this last story.

"But Dad," I replied, "That's the peace I've been telling you about for years!" That was part of a conversation I had with my father while he was in a nursing home a month after he had experienced renal failure and had awoken from a coma.

My father had a unique life of deliverances. When he was a child, he and his brother were thrown out of a third-story window to firefighters below. His mom threw them out – not figuratively but literally. They were so young to be tossed out the window; but their apartment was burning. I think his mother may have jumped, too!

Dad had other deliverances as well. During World War II, he was pulled off the gangplank of a ship destined for the Normandy invasion. The Army sent him to college instead. He did later serve in the Pacific campaign. In another incident, he escaped serious injury in an unexpected car crash. Having been diagnosed with diabetes when he was 42, and being a bit spacey, he was driving our new Dodge Dart in Brooklyn at night. It was our first new car. We always had used cars mainly because we could wreck them without too much remorse. Anyway, back to the story, he made a left-hand turn and ran into a taxi head-on and totaled the car. He got out of the car without a scratch.

In the late 70s, my father had another close call, this time a medical emergency. He had a gallstone lodged between his gall bladder and his liver. The doctors would not operate because of complications, and at the same time poisons from his liver were backing up into his blood stream. The doctors decided to put a scope down through his throat and stomach, through the gallbladder, and try to dislodge the stone. When they went down with the scope, the stone could not be found. It had disappeared. I had a book on my bookshelf called, *Who Moved the Stone,* by Frank Morrison. It discusses the options of who moved the stone away from Jesus' tomb. Was it Jewish parties, Roman soldiers, or God? My dad took the book and read it because he wanted to know who moved the gallstone from his bile duct.

We'll finish the story next time ....

### *"That's the Peace I've Been Telling You About"* (Isaiah 9:6)
### 12/31/10

In the early 1980s, my parents moved from Merrick, NY, to Massachusetts to be closer to my sister Dorrie and her family. One day, when my sister was visiting their rental, my dad collapsed, unconscious, in the kitchen. His heart had stopped. My sister, being a nurse, repositioned him to give him CPR; and, because of the sudden movement, his heart started pumping again. If she had not been there just then, he would have died. He then received a pacemaker.

In the early 1990s, after having lost a leg to diabetes, Dad went into a coma because of renal failure. He was immediately put on dialysis while still in the coma. My sister and mother had decided that they would wait 3 days; and if he did not come out of the coma, they would take him off dialysis. At the same time, we were praying here in California. He came out of his coma.

I went to visit him a few months later. He was living at the Jewish Home for the Aged in Worcester, MA. He was leading a group of amputees in a support group and complained that people were not attending. I told him not to be concerned about their attitudes because they "did not have a leg to stand on." I actually received my humor from him, so don't worry, he laughed at my comment.

I had a chance to talk to him about all the ways God had delivered him from near-death experiences and that it was miraculous that he was alive. He admitted to me that he knew that there was a "life-giving force" that was keeping him alive, and acknowledged that the prayers of everyone helped him. I asked him if I could pray with him, and he gave me permission. I prayed that my dad would be able to understand all the things that were happening to him and that he would be able to understand who *Yeshua*, Jesus, is. He said that my prayer was exactly what he would have wanted to pray; and then, in astonishment, he said he felt a tremendous peace. I said, "Dad, that's the peace I've been telling you and Mom and Dorrie about for years. People say that if Jesus is the Messiah, why didn't He bring peace? But He does. He brings peace to our hearts!" He then said he wanted to go to sleep, and I let him and went on my way. We did not talk of this exchange again; but when my dad died a year later and when I saw his body, he had a big smile on his face! I smiled as well and said, "Dad, you made it!"

We'll continue with the remainder of Chapter 9 next time!

### True World Peace (Isaiah 9:7)
4/19/11

Well, I think we've spent enough time exhaustively exploring Isaiah 9:6. Now it's time to move on to four months of verse 7! Just kidding. As mentioned, Leupold writes of Isaiah Chapter 9, verses 6 and 7, "It goes without saying that this is one of the clearest and most meaningful Messianic prophesies in the whole Old Testament" (p. 187).

Verse 7 describes the future of the child mentioned in verse 6: *There will be no end to the increase of His government or of peace.* As world members, we are in desperate search of one who will guide us out of our present daunting political and economic crises. To our demise, we will easily follow a counterfeit charismatic and charming leader who will promise peace and economic security, and we will follow this leader because we will believe the good feelings we will get from this figure's words. This person will speak our emotional language. It may be so powerful an emotion that logic will succumb to it. Instead of a promise of our deliverance, these words will be a sinister deception.

Despite the disastrous words and actions of this deceiving world leader, the true Messiah will bring about true world peace and security. He will sit upon the throne of David, and He will rule with *justice and righteousness* (verse 7). According to Leupold, the Justice will consist of "official pronouncements that are made in connection with His work," and the Righteousness will be "the quality that governs all that He personally does" (p. 187). *The zeal of the LORD of hosts will accomplish this* (verse 7).

Fascinating as it is, according to Keil and Delitzsch, the word for *zeal* can also be translated "jealousy." The word *kin'ah* in Hebrew literally means a "glowing fire." It is a jealousy that "burns." They explain that the Lord's jealousy will not allow His people to remain in the hands of ones who are sinister (Keil and Delitzsch, p. 165). He will fight for our well-being! He will establish a new Kingdom!

More next time.

### *They Wanted to Build Back Better (Isaiah 9:8-12)*

8/07/11

Again, it's been a long time, but I will continue to press on. The last time we completed verse 7 of Isaiah Chapter 9, so let's go through verses 8-12; then next time, verse 13; and finally verses 14-21 to complete the chapter.

Verses 8-12 bring us back from a view of Messiah's future reign to the current reality, a local condition (verse 8). Ephraim and Samaria, both comprising the northern kingdom of Israel, are saying *in pride and in arrogance of heart* (verse 9): *"The bricks have fallen down, but we will rebuild them with smooth stones; the sycamores have been cut down, but we will replace them with cedars"* (verse 10). According to Keil and Delitzsch, the poorest types of building material, dried brick and sycamores (only grown in the plains), will be replaced by the best. "More desirable and stately buildings would rise up in their place" (pp. 166 and 167).

My thoughts go to our beloved nation, which has experienced a myriad of powerful man-made and natural disasters recently. Our response has always been to rebuild and make things stronger; but these phenomena may become stronger than we will be able to resist, and then we will have to sincerely rely on the mercy of God for help. It will humble us to do so, but all we need to do is turn to Him.

So in response to Israel's persistent pride, the Lord will raise up other problems with a persistent stretched-out hand, until Israel returns to Him.

> *[11] Therefore the LORD raises against them adversaries from Rezin,*
> *And spurs their enemies on,*
> *[12] The Arameans on the east and the Philistines on the west;*
> *And they devour Israel with gaping jaws.*
> *In spite of all this, His anger does not turn away,*
> *And His hand is still stretched out.*

As our congregational leader would say immediately after delivering a not so "encouraging" message, "And now let's rise for the

Aaronic benediction, which ironically is a blessing." We'll look at verses 13-17 next time.

### Turn Toward or Turn Away? (Isaiah 9:13)

11/20/11

Again, it's been a long time, but I will continue to press on. Today, we will look at Isaiah 9, verse 13. Verse 13 makes a striking comment: *Yet the people do not turn back to Him.* The words *turn back* have the same meaning as "repent," but most people I know would not understand it if we told them to "repent." It's too religious or Christian a word. It brings out a lot of resentment for the legalism and hypocrisy of our congregations and has also a sense of self-righteousness. So, *turn back* makes more sense, and I recommend we use the term often. It really gives us two choices or directions. There is no middle ground. You either turn away or turn to Him.

I left out the phrase, *who struck them above.* Verse 13 reads: *Yet the people do not turn back to Him who struck them.* If we have a concept of God that is simply a wrathful God without considering His overwhelming love, this will also be a bad way to communicate. How could we, as children, turn back to a parent who is harsh, unmerciful, and abusive? We would want to run farther away. Our enemy would want us to view God in that way. So, as we read about God's judgment upon Israel, we need to look at it through the lens of a God who is Holy and hates sin but, at the same time, is a God who loves us and wants to get our attention. Isaiah 9 verse 13 concludes with, *Nor do they seek the LORD of hosts.* Seek Him and you will find Him.

When I was in college, in the 1970s, I volunteered to help clean houses in Wilkes-Barre, PA, after a hurricane and subsequent flood ruined many homes. I saw messages painted on houses which read, "Where was God?" In my mind, God was getting our attention and saying, "I'm waking you up from slumber! Turn to Me!" Let's look at verses 14-17 next time.

### Unreliable in Many Ways (Isaiah 9:14-21)
12/09/11

Today we will finish Isaiah Chapter 9, starting with verse 14. This verse reveals that the Lord will cut off from Israel *head and tail, palm branch and bulrush,* in one day. Verses 15 and 16 give the explanation. *The head is the elder and honorable man,* and the tail is *the prophet who teaches falsehood* (verse 15). Leupold writes that "the first quality of any leader should be his utter reliability" (p. 192). On the contrary, here the leaders have led their people astray, and those who were led astray allowed it to happen to them. Keil and Delitzsch put it this way: "The chiefs of the nation were the head of the national body; and behind, like a wagging dog's tail, sat the false prophets with their flatteries of the people" (p. 168).

Verse 17 shows the result of turning away from the Lord: *Therefore the Lord does not take pleasure in their young men, nor does He have pity on their orphans and their widows.* The nature of our Lord, our Father, is to care for the fatherless and the widow. He is very concerned for the orphan. He has tremendous compassion that you can feel. He is concerned also for our every need. Maybe we can say that He is extremely pained to have to come to this point where judgment must come. God is holy and is love. He loves us but cannot live with our sin. We need to turn to Him to be cleansed, and then we can have and feel His fellowship and love.

Verse 18 explains: *For wickedness burns like a fire; it consumes briars and thorns; it even sets the thickets of the forest aflame, and they roll upward in a column of smoke.* Verse 19a continues: *By the fury of the LORD of hosts the land is burned up, and the people are like fuel for the fire; no man spares his brother.* The wickedness of the people will be as a fuel that will feed and spread a daunting and powerful wildfire. Leupold says it this way, "Wickedness blazes on powerfully" (p. 194). Verses 20 and 21 continue with this theme. Israel's wickedness will not satisfy them, and they will be persistent in their appetite for evil in a way that will bring horrific consequences.

We in Southern California can see the aftermath of wildfires: ruined homes with only a foundation remaining, blackened hilltops, leafless trees, charred bark on the remains of tree stumps, and a quiet and desolate loneliness.

In Chapter 10, we will begin to see that the desolate forest will show a spark of hope; and in Chapter 11, a small shoot will rise from the blackened landscape.

We'll explore the idea of hope next time.

# Isaiah Chapter 10 Assyria's Conquests and Assyria's Demise

### 2/20/12

"I have just read Chapter 10." ___ yes

We begin Chapter 10 with an array of thoughts. I have been reading this complicated chapter over and over again and find it to be filled with different approaches to the same problem. The Assyrians will be used as a tool to judge Israel. God will then judge the Assyrians for their arrogance in judging Israel. And, finally, as we enter into Chapter 11, Israel will be restored.

### Are We Protecting the Needy, Poor, Widows, and Orphans? (Isaiah 10:1-4)

Verses 1 and 2 decry the unjust decrees of rulers who deny and ignore the rights and needs of the needy, poor, widows, and orphans. They are "crowded away from justice rather than helped to obtain it," says Leupold (p.198).

I remember a professor at my old college, many years ago, who was decrying Christianity because Jesus said, *"For the poor you always have with you,..."* He was assuming that *Yeshua*, Jesus, was teaching that the poor were an unavoidable part of any society, and that it was okay. In contrast, though, *Yeshua* had great compassion and respect for the poor. He was the Good Shepherd who cared for His sheep, rich or poor. Here in Isaiah, we see the Lord putting the responsibility on the rulers for the condition of the poor. As Leupold asserts, "Sins like these cry out to high heaven for vengeance" (p. 198). God's heart is always toward the needy, poor, widows, and orphans because He is a Father, and He is jealous for their well being.

So, in verse 3, a day of reckoning is coming as if an ominous storm were brewing on the far horizon. And when this phenomenon comes, what can one do to escape it? Where can one flee for help? As the passage asks, *To whom will you flee for help? And where will you leave your wealth?* (verse 3b). In this situation, you cannot put your possessions in a safe deposit box or in a Swiss bank. You can't even put them in your tomb in hope of a future life with them. You have to leave all your stuff behind. Verse 4 continues that you cannot hide behind other prisoners when taken captive in the war, meaning the war with the Assyrian army, or hide behind other corpses on the field of battle. So, the best thing to do is to prepare to meet your Maker, your God. Reach out to Him and He will reach out to you. Seek Him and you will find Him.

More next time.

### The Rod of My Anger (Isaiah 10:5-10)
8/07/13

Continuing, verse 5 speaks of Assyria as *the rod of My anger,* and a symbol of God's fury. We cannot understand God's anger toward sin unless we understand His love. In reverse, we cannot understand His love unless we can understand His holiness and His anger toward sin. He wants the best for us, and it makes Him furious when we are harming ourselves or others and being unjust toward our fellow man. It comes to a point when things are so out of control that He has to intervene.

Verse 6 continues that it is the mission of Assyria *to capture booty and to seize plunder* and *to trample them* [sons of Israel] *down like mud in the streets*. These are war words. That's what happens during war. It will be a total devastation, a thorough one.

Verse 7 reveals that the Assyrians had some idea that God was using them to act as His agent to destroy Israel, but the pride of Assyria will be its demise. Says Leupold, "Lust of conquest dominated their thinking" (p. 201).

Verses 8 and 9 reveal that the thoughts of the Assyrian king were that "none of the cities he is minded to take will be able to resist effectually" (Leupold, p. 201). Regarding verse 10 Leupold continues, "an Assyrian victory was proof that their gods were stronger than those of their enemies" (p. 202). From Assyria's perspective, their nation's idols excelled over those of Israel.

More next time ....

### Pride and Prejudice (Isaiah 10:10-14)

10/05/14

It's a tough one to continue. I've got the information, but the motivation is daunting. Let not one be a teacher.

We continue with Chapter 10, verses 10 and 11. As mentioned last time, the Assyrian king's opinion was that Assyria's gods were stronger than the gods of their enemies. He may not have understood the special attributes of the God of Israel, and may not have known that the religion of Israel detested worship of other gods. He was just clueless.

Verse 12 continues with a successive use of the word *of*, in order to emphasize His distaste for the pride of the king of Assyria and that of his nation. The Lord is speaking now personally, *"I will punish the fruit of the arrogant heart of the king of Assyria and the pomp of his haughtiness."* Leupold put it this way: "His [the Assyrian king's] pride is superb" (p. 202). According to *The American Heritage College Dictionary,* there are a lot of different definitions for *superb.* One is "majestic and imposing." Verses 13 and 14 continue in this theme with the king of Assyria boasting, *"By the power of my hand and by my wisdom I did this, for I have understanding; and I removed the boundaries of the peoples, and plundered their treasures, and like a mighty man I brought down their inhabitants,"* and the list goes on and on. He does not know that he's in for a big surprise.

As we look at our world today, it's the same. We think we can dictate how the world is to be organized. We can conduct our regime changes without a thought, and we can even dictate to Israel how to coexist with its neighbors. And also, we think we are in charge of our personal state as well. Better to be humble and hand over our lives and life's situations to our Lord.

### A Wasting Disease, A Consuming Fire (Isaiah 10:15-19)
11/27/15

Well, it's been a year. Shall we continue with verse 15?

It's ridiculous for the guitar to think that it is creating the music or for the drum to think it is making the beat. It's ridiculous for the axe to think that it is controlling the wood chopper. If I may quote Keil and Delitzsch, "A stick is wood and nothing more. In itself, it is an absolutely motionless thing" (p.175). In verse 15 of Chapter 10, the king of Assyria thinks that he is the one who is conquering Israel; but, no, it isn't he directing his own path.

Verse 16 continues that the Lord will send a *wasting disease among his stout warriors* or "well fed" warriors (the Assyrians). Keil and Delitzsch call it a "galloping consumption" (p. 175). And this is indeed what happened after much prayer and intercession during Hezekiah's reign: *Then it happened that night that the angel of the LORD went out and struck 185,000 in the camp of the Assyrians; and when men rose early in the morning, behold, all of them were dead* (2 Kings 19:35).

Some other examples of this sort can be found in Leviticus Chapter 26, verse 16, *"'I will appoint over you a sudden terror, consumption and fever that will waste away the eyes and cause the soul to pine away'";* and in Deuteronomy 28:22, *"The LORD will smite you with consumption and with fever and with inflammation and with fiery heat and with the sword and with blight and with mildew."* Doesn't sound like very much fun.

The second part of verse 16, *A fire will be kindled like a burning flame,* refers to the sounds a fire makes as it works its way through the wood. Keil and Delitzsch describe it as the "crackling, sputtering and hissing" of fire (p. 175). If you can visualize this, that's how the Assyrian army will experience this *consumption*.

Verses 17 and 18 indicate that there is no distinction. The thorns and briars represent the lower parts of society, and the glory of the forest represents the higher levels (Leupold, p. 206). As Leupold continues, "The Assyrians will be found to be as frail as other mortals …. The arrogant will be brought low" (p. 206).

Verse 19 concludes, *And the rest of the trees of his forest will be so small in number that a child could write them down.* Only a few in the Assyrian force will have escaped the judgment; and, at the same time, as we'll see in Chapter 11, a new *shoot* will arise indicating a hope in the future for Israel.

### On What or Whom Do We Depend? (Isaiah 10:20-23)

2/2/17

Well, it took the experience of food poisoning together with the flu to get me to write this next portion. I had the feeling of dying in bed, shaking, nausea, vomiting, being unable to stand or keep my balance. Just to let you know that my wife, Caty, was wonderful in helping me through this time. I'm a little better now and so I decided it was time to continue. After all, I am approaching 65 and realize that I have only 20 years or so available for me to finish this work!

So we continue. Of course, we depend on our jobs, the stock market, and our doctors. Yet it is important to note that we need to get the idea into our heads that we really depend on God to help us, not man or things, or allies for that matter. I once had a wise doctor who admitted that he did not have much to do with one's recovery from an illness and noted that the human body is so complex, with miniscule cells all working in different ways, that he could only influence them to work; but the rest was up to the miraculous.

Look at Israel today. This tiny country has had to depend on the West to help her in every war and in every crisis. Its neighboring countries always ask, "Why does the West help her?" But ultimately, Israel needs to rely on the Lord, not man. When we ponder how Israel has survived through these times, we have to realize that God has helped her. She may take the credit for valiant military accomplishments, but even those warriors in the midst of battle admit that something miraculous had occurred.

Here in Chapter 10, verses 20-23, we see that Israel's *remnant*, those who escaped because of their faith, will never again rely on the one who struck them (Egypt, Assyria, and in the future, the West) (verse 20), but will rely only on the Lord, the Holy One of Israel. I refer to the psalm that says, *Some boast in chariots, and some in horses; but we will boast in the name of the LORD, our God* (Psalm 20:7). Israel will realize that God is her only hope and will return to Him (verse 21). Even though Israel's large number is referred to as *the sand of the sea* (verse 22), only a small portion will in fact return. As for Assyria and the rest, great destruction is appointed for them. It was pre-determined (verse 23).

### There Will Always Be a Remnant (Isaiah 10:21-23)
### 4/21/17

Well, it's been only 2 months! Shall we continue? Chapter 10 mentions a *remnant* in verses 21-22:

> [21] *A remnant will return, the remnant of Jacob, to the mighty God.*
>
> [22] *For though your people, O Israel, may be like the sand of the sea,*
> *Only a remnant within them will return;*
> *A destruction is determined, overflowing with righteousness.*

The idea of a *remnant* is very humbling. I remember many ages ago being a young believer and a student at Fairleigh Dickinson University (FDU). I was a security guard for a brief stint and would live in this little guard house at night and let people in and out of the campus. (I didn't really live there, but it did feel like I was in a little prison of my own.) A fellow guard named Charlie was a Jehovah's Witness. He was an older guy who had little emotion and was convinced he had the truth. The campus priest was a great guy, but at the same time was known to enter the campus a little tipsy, uh, I mean drunk. The protestant minister on campus told me he used to be a Bible-believing pastor but now had more of an open mind. The Jewish students on campus considered me a traitor, and the Christian students thought I was wacko. So, I felt I was the righteous bearer of truth in that environment, and I was honored to be so. The problem was that it made me feel special and in a way superior. At that time I needed to feel special, and any psychologist would point to that as the reason I had chosen such a radical path. I had not yet learned the truth that I had the same potential as everyone else to be a heretic, so to speak. So I was part of the *remnant*, but was really *egoista* about it. That's Spanish for one who looks down on others.

Yes, I was proud and egotistical, but in time I realized that being a part of the *remnant* is a humbling experience. We all have the potential to walk away from our faith, and it is God who keeps us faithful. It is also God who opens our eyes in order for us to be able to see His truth. So, let's all be humble and be thankful whenever we can do anything to honor Him.

### *A New Perspective (Isaiah 10:24)*
6/05/17

Well, it's now a day before my 65th birthday. I'm not going to retire for another year. I know the powers that be want me to retire ASAP; but, just in spite, I'll wait one more year in order to inflict more *tsuris* (trouble) on my enemies …

Back to the passage at hand, verse 24 thunders, *Therefore thus says the Lord GOD of hosts, "O My people who dwell in Zion, do not fear the Assyrian who strikes you with the rod and lifts up his staff against you, the way Egypt did."* I learned recently that *hosts* means "armies." *Thus says the Lord GOD of armies.* It's tough for our contemporary Western minds to comprehend that God is a warrior God. We want God to simply be a God of peace and love. We cannot see with our practical eyes that there is a tremendous spiritual war going on all around us.

In this chapter, as above, and in Chapters 11 and 59, Isaiah talks of spiritual protection from the forces about us using military terms:

> Isaiah 11:5: *Also righteousness will be the belt about His loins, and faithfulness the belt about His waist.*

> Isaiah 59:17: *And He put on righteousness like a breastplate, and a helmet of salvation on His head; and He put on garments of vengeance for clothing, and wrapped Himself with zeal as a mantle.*

The *Brit Chadashah,* the New Testament, refers to this same imagery in the Book of Ephesians, Chapter 6:

> [13] *Therefore, take up the full armor of God, that you may be able to resist in the evil day, and having done everything, to stand firm.* [14] *Stand firm therefore, HAVING GIRDED YOUR LOINS WITH TRUTH, and HAVING PUT ON THE BREASTPLATE OF RIGHTEOUSNESS,* [15] *and having shod YOUR FEET WITH THE PREPARATION OF THE GOSPEL OF PEACE;* [16] *in addition to all, taking up the shield of faith with which you will be able to extinguish all the*

*flaming missiles of the evil one.* ¹⁷ *And take THE HELMET OF SALVATION, and the sword of the Spirit, which is the word of God.*

The concept of resisting evil is not new. Those who attack us, snub us, talk evil of us, etc., *yada, yada, yada* – you get the picture – are not the ones who need to really concern us. From a spiritual perspective, we can shudder that these individuals have been used as a tool to discourage us; and they are not even aware of it. That's why we need to view our personal and political situations with a spiritual perspective. The Lord told Israel not to fear. They would be delivered from Assyria the same way they were delivered from Egypt many years prior.

### *Do Not Fear (Isaiah 10:24-26)*

1/07/20 (current events)

Well, it's now the year 2020! I remember *1984*, the classic by George Orwell. In that great book, Big Brother was always watching us. So, it has come to pass in 2020. Any cell phone can be tracked and any bank account recorded by the powers that be. I also remember the movie, *2001, A Space Odyssey* where Hal, the computer, took over operations of a spaceship heading for Mars. (Hal, by the way, is IBM when you add one letter to H, A, and L.) Anyway, we are now planning to go to Mars, and cyber warfare is paramount.

I have now been retired from teaching ESL (English as a Second Language) for almost 6 months. I was in that profession for 21 years! I miss it, and I don't miss it. Now, I am tuning pianos full time, also a long-term occupation I have kept my hand in part time up until now. When I was teaching, I could be a stand-up comedian with my students. They may not have understood my humor, but at least I had fun. Now, I just stare at a piano and try to listen to it. The piano doesn't understand my humor either!

Oh well, back to the study!

Continuing in verse 24, notice how it says, *"O My people."* It shows God's love for Israel (Leupold, p. 209). When quoting God's words, "it is not the prophet's intention to threaten and terrify, but to comfort and encourage," writes Keil and Delitzsch (p. 177).

The Scripture continues, *"... do not fear the Assyrian who strikes you with the rod and lifts up his staff against you, the way Egypt did."* "The intention of the Assyrian will be deadly," says Leupold (p. 209). Isaiah further refers to the way Egypt treated the people of Israel; but the more the Egyptians oppressed Israel, the better off Israel became. Leupold continues, "They [the Assyrians] were indeed sent as a rod of punishment against Israel, but they cruelly overdid their part enough to arouse God's wrath" (p. 209). So, verse 25 continues with the thought that the Assyrian attack will not last very much longer.

Verse 26 mentions Midian and the rock of Oreb. The story of Midian is in Judges 7:25 where Gideon, with 300 men, 300 pitchers, 300 torches, and 300 trumpets, gave the impression that there were 300,000 Israelites ready to advance on the city. This perception created such panic and confusion among the Midianites that they literally fought against each other instead of against Israel. The rod of Moses is also mentioned in verse 26. Egypt, with overwhelming numbers, could not recapture the people of Israel because they could not see. The Cloud by Day hid Israel, and Israel was able to enter the Red Sea on dry land and make it to the other side safely. Then, when the Egyptian chariots entered the dry land of the Red Sea, the sea closed in on them. So, in the same way, via what seems to us as impossible, Israel will be delivered from the Assyrians.

We will continue with verse 27 next time, and try to decide if we're dealing with *anointing oil* or *fat*. We'll see that commentators differ on that one ...

### Tremendous Hope (Isaiah 10:27)

3/28/20 In the midst of the Coronavirus Outbreak

The New American Standard Bible translates verse 27 as: *So it will be in that day, that his burden will be removed from your shoulders and his yoke from your neck, and the yoke will be broken because of fatness.* Other translations read: *the yoke will be broken because of the* **anointing** or because of *the* **anointing oil.** The word in question is the Hebrew word *shemen*, which can be translated both ways. When discussing whether the yoke is broken because of the fat or because of the anointing oil, the result is the same: The yoke was broken. The image refers again back to Israel's slavery in Egypt. The Egyptians were the ones driving Israel, their beast of burden. The fact that the yoke will be broken is a sign of tremendous hope for freedom for Israel. Verse 27 points to future freedom from the new oppressor, Assyria.

When taking the interpretation in verse 27 that the neck will grow so thick and fat that it will literally burst the yoke open, the indication is that the natural result is reversed. Keil and Delitzsch quote the revered Jewish sage Kimchi as saying, "In most cases, the yoke creates a wound in the fat flesh of the ox by pressure or friction, but here the very opposite occurs, and the fatness of the ox leads to the destruction of the yoke" (p. 178).

So, the Lord was going to create faith and persistence in the Jewish people. Their God-given, undeterred determination will break the yoke of the Assyrians. The assumption is that the people of Jerusalem understood that it was God who delivered them and not themselves. That is in great contrast to the average Israeli's attitude after winning the Six-Day War in June of 1967. It was a preemptive Israeli victory preventing an imminent invasion of Israel by Egypt, Syria, and Jordan. Israel basically took the credit, though I'm sure there were many in Israel who knew that it was divine intervention that won that war.

Others have translated the passage in verse 27 to read, *because of the anointing,* or *because of the anointing oil.* These are references to the intervention of the Messiah as the *anointing* or the intervention of the Holy Spirit as the *anointing oil.*

At this point you may be asking, "Why do Bible versions translate passages differently?" First of all, the Hebrew manuscript is pure. When you compare the Isaiah fragments found in the Dead Sea Scrolls, they vary only slightly from the Hebrew texts we have today. So, the difference lies in how a translator's biases affect the way they present a passage when relating it to another language and culture. Of course, Jewish translations will come from a different perspective than Christian translations when going from the original language to a different language, such as English. Our goal is to find an accurate translation without biases. As the saying goes, "When the plain sense of Scripture makes common sense, seek no other sense ..." (David L. Cooper, n.d.).

To see a list of Bible versions and how they translate *shemen,* please refer to Endnote [1], p. 139.

In order to grasp the emotion at that time, think of the fear we are experiencing today because of the invasion of the Coronavirus. To us, it is a taste of what those living in Jerusalem would have felt when anticipating the imminent invasion of the Assyrian army.

The Assyrian messengers were outside the city walls claiming that they were the instruments of the Jewish God in order to judge the city. Isaiah 36:10 states the words of Rabshakeh, the Assyrian representative, to Hezekiah, *"And have I now come up without the LORD's approval against this land to destroy it? The LORD said to me, 'Go up against this land, and destroy it.'"*

How do you fight against God's will? In the same way, we at this time may be thinking that the Coronavirus is one of the birth pangs mentioned in Matthew 24, one of the signs of the soon coming of the Messiah: *For nation shall rise against nation, and kingdom against kingdom: there shall be famines, and pestilences, and earthquakes, in divers places* (Matthew 24:7 KJV). Some translations only say *famines and earthquakes,* but the idea is the same.

How then do you resist God's will? Well, I'm realizing that the Holy Spirit, the *Ruach Ha Khodesh,* is presently encouraging us to pray for the defeat of this virus and wanting us to believe that our prayers will be answered.

King Hezekiah did not hesitate to ask for God's help and did not resign himself to the judgment of God on Judah. We see his story developed later, in Isaiah Chapters 36 and 37. The Assyrians were at the edge of Jerusalem, and as mentioned before, they believed that they were the instrument and power God would use to judge Judah.

Hezekiah could have reasoned, "How do you resist God's will?" He could have despaired and grieved at this threatening statement. Instead, Hezekiah went immediately to the Lord. Through the words of the prophet Isaiah, quoted below (Isaiah 37:36). God's message to

Hezekiah was to be encouraged that He has worked powerfully in the past and He will bring tremendous deliverance now. As a result of King Hezekiah's prayers, God mercifully intervened; and the following transpired:

> *"Then the angel of the LORD went out, and struck 185,000 in the camp of the Assyrians; and when men arose early in the morning, behold, all of these were dead." (Isaiah 37:36)*

We can be assured that the saying, "Prayer changes things," is true when we come before the God of the universe.

### Assyria's March Abruptly Shut Down (Isaiah 10:28-32)

4/04/20 In the midst of the Coronavirus Outbreak

Now that the whole story of Jerusalem's deliverance has been given away, we can backtrack and examine the steps that Sennacherib, the general of the Assyrian army, took to approach Jerusalem. Note that Isaiah was writing in the historical present, which means the actual invasion had not happened yet. He was "vividly describing an event that lies in the future" (Leupold, p. 211).

The victories of the Assyrian army are recorded in verses 28-32. According to Leupold (p. 211), the account listed here is a poetic one, naming conquered city after conquered city, not as a "matter of fact" list but one with intensified emotion. It was written as if you were reading newspaper headlines every day, "war bulletin style" (p. 211). Just to note: there are other passages in the *Tanakh* (the Old Testament) where this step by step style is also employed such as in Zechariah 9:1-10.

Keil and Delitzsch describe the march this way:

> The prophet's address moved on at a hurried, strong pace; then it halted and seemed as if it were, panting with anxiety; it now breaks forth in a dactylic movement like a long rolling thunder. The hostile army stands in front of Jerusalem, like a broad dense forest (p. 181).

Leupold writes, "The city is within grasp and all but taken when the account is significantly interrupted. That is as far as it ever got. The danger was acute. The fall of the city was imminent. Her doom was sealed. Yet, that last step never became a reality" (p. 212).

Interestingly enough, according to the editors of *The New Bible Atlas* (p. 51):

> The catastrophic outcome of Sennacherib's campaign was naturally suppressed in the Assyrian account which ends, instead, on a victorious note listing the tribute received in Nineveh.

### *A Child Can Write Them Down (Isaiah 10:19-34)*

4/14/20 In the midst of the Coronavirus Outbreak

We are approaching the surge or peak of the Coronavirus pandemic. After that, we will still have to wear face masks and gloves for a few more months and still practice social distancing. I was beginning to wonder if we would ever again shake hands or give and receive hugs.

Back to Isaiah 10! The end of the chapter explains that this "broad dense forest" is to be cut down. The forest is compared to the majestic cedars of Lebanon, of such quality wood that Solomon requested of Hiram, king of Tyre, that it be used to build the Temple (1 Kings 5:6). Leupold explains, "Assyria is that forest. The Lord is the woodsman. The mighty and proud trees are seen to crash one after another. Blows of the axe have taken the place of the din of battle. The net result is the same. Assyria will meet with a catastrophic overthrow" (p. 212).

And referring back to verse 19, *"And the rest of the trees of his [the king of Assyria's] forest will be so small in number that a child could write them down,"* but the imagery in verse 19 is referring to the fire and fury of the Lord which consumed the forest.

Isaiah 37:33-36 reads:

> [33] *"Therefore, thus says the LORD concerning the king of Assyria, 'He shall not come to this city, or shoot an arrow there; neither shall he come before it with a shield, nor throw up a siege mound against it.* [34] *By the way that he came, by the same he will return, and he will not come to this city,' declares the LORD.* [35] *'For I will defend this city to save it for My own sake and for My servant David's sake.'"*

> [36] *Then the angel of the LORD went out, and struck 185,000 in the camp of the Assyrians; and when men arose early in the morning, behold, all of these were dead.*

If you wish to look it up, the Book of 2 Kings, Chapter 19, verses 32-35 mirror the same passage verbatim, copying the words of Isaiah's prophesy.

Fruchtenbaum makes this statement concerning the contrast between the last verse of Chapter 10 and the first verse of Chapter 11. "While in that verse, the Assyrian forest is viewed as having been cut down forever, the stump of Israel would bring forth a shoot, meaning it would bring forth new life" (p. 156).

We'll explore this as we enter Chapter 11 next time.

# ENDNOTE: Chapter 10

[1]Provided here is a list of Bible translations of Chapter 10, verse 27, related to page 133.

> *So it will be in that day, that his burden will be removed from your shoulders and his yoke from your neck, and the yoke will be broken because of **fatness** [shemen].* (New American Standard Bible)

Some translators have interpreted the term ***shemen*** to mean "physical fatness," others "anointing oil," and still others "oil" or "ointment," as shown below.

### Fat

American Standard Bible: **by reason of <u>fatness</u>**.
New American Standard Bible: **because of <u>fatness</u>**.
New International Version: **because you have grown so <u>fat</u>**.
The English Standard Version*: **because of the <u>fat</u>**.

*The English Standard Version includes a footnote saying: "The meaning of the Hebrew is unclear."

### Anointing Oil

King James Version: **because of the <u>anointing</u>**.
Darby Translation: **because of the <u>anointing</u>**.

### Other Interpretations

The following translations do not provide a way to come to a definite conclusion:

Douay-Rheims 1899 American Edition: **and the yoke shall putrefy at the presence of the <u>oil</u>**.

Living Bible**: **He will break the yoke of slavery off their necks and destroy it as decreed.**

**The translation includes a footnote saying: "literally: **because of <u>ointment</u>**. Some see here a reference to Messiah, the Anointed One."

As mentioned before, the fact that the yoke will be broken is a sign of tremendous hope for the freedom of Israel.

# Isaiah Chapter 11   Tremendous Hope for the Future

5/23/20 Still in the Midst of the Coronavirus Outbreak

"I have just read Chapter 11." ___ yes

## *A Humble Beginning (Isaiah 11:1)*

We have apparently passed the "surge" or "peak" of the Coronavirus pandemic. Things are looking better. Our governor says it's a matter of weeks, not months, when some restrictions will be lifted. We're wondering, though, if some of this is a political concern rather than a health concern.

As we begin Isaiah, Chapter 11, it's important to understand that the Hebrew Scriptures indicate that Messiah comes twice: the first time Messiah comes as a humble servant and the second time as a reigning king. Verse 1 talks of Messiah as the humble servant; and then beginning with verse 2, there is a description of a future kingdom on Earth with Messiah reigning as king.

Jumping into the next part of the study, Chapter 11, we are confronted with the image of a small shoot springing up from the stump or stem of a tree that has been cut down. Verse 1 reads: *Then a shoot will spring from the stem of Jesse, and a branch from his roots will bear fruit.*

The tree of interest is not one of the trees from the forest mentioned in Chapter 10. Instead, this tree is a symbol of the Messianic line of David that has declined to such insignificance that it has been reduced to a tree stump. Fruchtenbaum describes it this way:

> The stump belonged to Jesse, David's father. When one thinks of Jesse, [one] thinks of a shepherd in the small village of Bethlehem. When one thinks of David, [one] thinks of a king. The point Isaiah was making is that a time would come when the glorious House of David would be reduced to nothing but the stump of a felled tree. At this point, the Davidic dynasty would have lost all of its power and glory. When the mighty House of David would be reduced to what it was in Jesse's day, not in David's day, Messiah would come (p. 156).

**Degrees of Difficulty**

6/09/20

We are still in the midst of the Coronavirus outbreak and now are dealing with the murder of an innocent African American man by a deranged police officer and the ensuing demonstrations. Every sinister group has tried to take advantage of sincere demonstrations in order to advance their own cause. I wonder if our nation will be the same after all this division and violence. Will we be able to rebound? It will only be by God's grace and intervention.

Shall we continue?

This opening verse in Isaiah Chapter 11 contains three Hebrew words – *choter, geza,* and *netzer* – that vary in meaning from translation to translation:

> *Then a **choter** will spring from the **geza** of Jesse, and a **netzer** from his roots will bear fruit.*

*Choter* has been translated as "TWIG," "SHOOT" and "ROD."

*Geza* has been translated as "STEM," "STUMP" and "STOCK."

*Netzer* has been translated as "BRANCH" and "SHOOT."

From what I have been able to gather, each translator expresses the meaning of these various Hebrew words according to what they believe is the degree of difficulty that a shoot would be able to appear. For example, it would be more difficult for a shoot to grow from a root or stump than from a stem. For a more detailed look at how different Bible versions translate these three terms, please refer to the Appendix where I have added further information for those of you with inquiring minds to examine.

We can see another example of Messiah's humble beginning later on in the Book of Isaiah, Chapter 53, verses 1 and 2:

> [1] *Who has believed our message?*
> *And to whom has the arm of the LORD been revealed?*
> [2] *For he grew up before Him like a tender* **shoot** *[yonek]*,
> *And like a root out of parched ground; ...*

Here in Isaiah 53, verse 2, the Hebrew word in question is the word *yonek*. According to Brown, Driver and Briggs, *yonek* can be translated "young plant, sapling (sucker)" (p. 413).

Isaiah 53, verse 2, continues the description of this humble figure:

> *... He has no stately form or majesty*
> *That we should look upon Him,*
> *Nor appearance that we should be attracted to Him.*

Isaiah 53, verse 3a, follows with this description:

> *He was despised and forsaken of men,*
> *A man of sorrows and acquainted with grief.*

Traditionally, the figure in Isaiah 53 is understood by Jewish scholars to be Israel, the nation that has suffered throughout the ages. Yet, when you see that the Isaiah 53 figure is introduced as a ***tender shoot*** and you compare that with Isaiah Chapter 11:1 where the shoot comes from the Messianic line of David, you can't help but see that the figure in Isaiah 53 is indeed the Messiah.

If you will, please read Isaiah Chapter 53 before continuing on with the study:

### ISAIAH 53
### - The Suffering Servant

*[1] Who has believed our message?*
*And to whom has the arm of the LORD been revealed?*

*[2] For He grew up before Him like a tender shoot,*
*And like a root out of parched ground;*
*He has no stately form or majesty*
*That we should look upon Him,*
*Nor appearance that we should be attracted to Him.*

*[3] He was despised and forsaken of men,*
*A man of sorrows, and acquainted with grief;*
*And like one from whom men hide their face,*
*He was despised, and we did not esteem Him.*

*⁴ Surely our griefs He Himself bore,*
*And our sorrows He carried;*
*Yet we ourselves esteemed Him stricken,*
*Smitten of God, and afflicted.*

*⁵ But He was pierced through for our transgressions,*
*He was crushed for our iniquities;*
*The chastening for our well-being fell upon Him,*
*And by His scourging we are healed.*

*⁶ All of us like sheep have gone astray,*
*Each of us has turned to his own way;*
*But the LORD has caused the iniquity of us all*
*To fall on Him.*

*⁷ He was oppressed and He was afflicted,*
*Yet He did not open His mouth;*
*Like a lamb that is led to slaughter,*
*And like a sheep that is silent before its shearers,*
*So He did not open His mouth.*

*⁸ By oppression and judgment He was taken away;*
*And as for His generation, who considered*
*That He was cut off out of the land of the living,*
*For the transgression of my people to whom the stroke was due?*

⁹ His grave was assigned with wicked men,
Yet He was with a rich man in His death,
Because He had done no violence,
Nor was there any deceit in His mouth.

¹⁰ But the LORD was pleased
To crush Him, putting Him to grief;
If He would render Himself as a guilt offering,
He will see His offspring,
He will prolong His days,
And the good pleasure of the LORD will prosper in His hand.

¹¹ As a result of the anguish of His soul,
He will see it and be satisfied;
By His knowledge the Righteous One,
My Servant, will justify the many,
As He will bear their iniquities.

¹² Therefore, I will allot Him a portion with the great,
And He will divide the booty with the strong;
Because He poured out Himself to death,
And was numbered with the transgressors;
Yet He Himself bore the sin of many,
And interceded for the transgressors.

## A Persistent Life (Isaiah 11:2)

6/19/20

Today, my dear wife's beloved brother died. Our hope is in the Lord's life-giving words, *"... I came that they might have life, and that they might have it abundantly"* (John 10:10b). We are very sad, but we know Moises is now at peace in the Lord's love and presence.

At my mother's funeral in 1996, I asked the rabbi to read Isaiah 61:1-3. It follows:

> *¹ The Spirit of the Lord GOD is upon me,*
> *Because the LORD has appointed me*
> *To bring good news to the afflicted;*
> *He has sent me to bind up the brokenhearted,*
> *To proclaim liberty to the captives,*
> *And freedom to prisoners;*
>
> *² To proclaim the favorable year of the LORD,*
> *And the day of vengeance of our God;*
> *To comfort all who mourn,*
>
> *³ To grant those who mourn in Zion,*
> *Giving them a garland instead of ashes,*
> *The oil of gladness instead of mourning,*
> *The mantle of praise instead of a spirit of fainting.*
> *So they will be called oaks of righteousness,*
> *The planting of the LORD, that He may be glorified.*

I specifically wanted this passage read because *Yeshua*, Jesus, quoted this same passage in the synagogue of His day and then said, *"Today this Scripture has been fulfilled in your hearing"* (Luke 4:21).

It is very common over time that a paved surface will crack and a small plant will appear growing from that crack. In the same way, God always brings light and life out of darkness and death. It is our hope. For example, look at Job Chapter 14, verses 7-9.

> [7] *For there is hope for a tree,*
> *When it is cut down, that it will sprout again*
> *And its shoots will not fail.*
> [8] *"Though its roots grow old in the ground,*
> *And its stump dies in the dry soil.*
> [9] *At the scent of water it will flourish*
> *And put forth sprigs like a plant.*

### The Seven-Branched Menorah (Isaiah 11:2)

6/24/20

The pain of Moises' passing is really sinking in. He was a great and well-accomplished man who always wanted to help others in life. He was also my friend. What makes his passing so hard is that it was so sudden.

Continuing in Isaiah 11, verse 2, we can find some of the attributes of the Messiah:

> *And the Spirit of the LORD will rest on Him,*
> *The spirit of wisdom and understanding,*
> *The spirit of counsel and strength,*
> *The spirit of knowledge and the fear of the LORD.*

If you will look at it this way, we have here a picture of the seven-branched menorah located in the Tabernacle. The center branch stands for the Spirit of the Lord with three pairs of Spirit branches on the sides representing the attributes of the Spirit given in this verse: wisdom and understanding, counsel and strength, and knowledge *and fear of the LORD*.

Other examples of the seven Spirits of God are noted in the Book of Revelation, the last book of the *Brit Chadashah*, the New Testament, which talks of the last days:

> *And from the throne proceed flashes of lightning and sounds and peals of thunder. And there were seven lamps of fire burning before the throne, which are the seven Spirits of God. (Revelation 4:5)*

> *And I saw between the throne (with the four living creatures) and the elders a Lamb standing, as if slain, having seven horns and seven eyes, which are the seven Spirits of God, sent out into all the earth. (Revelation 5:6)*

According to Keil and Delitzsch (p. 182), each pair of branches has a unique quality:

*Wisdom and understanding* stands for "intellectual life."

*Counsel and strength* indicates "practical life."

Finally, *knowledge and fear of the LORD* means "a direct relation to God."

*Wisdom* in Hebrew is *chokmah*. It is "the power of discerning the nature of things through the appearance" (Keil and Delitzsch, p. 183). It is the "capacity for comprehensive judgment coupled with the ability to put to practical use the insight that is enjoyed" (Leupold, p. 217). "It refers to administrative wisdom. Messiah would possess the ability to render right decisions at the right time so that they may be acted upon" (Fruchtenbaum, p. 159).

The word for *understanding* in Hebrew is *binah*. It is "the power of discerning the differences of things in their appearance" (Keil and Delitzsch, p. 183). It is "being able to decide between various possibilities with which a person may be confronted and to choose the most advantageous course under the circumstances, ... the ability to solve problems" (Leupold, p. 217).

*Counsel* in Hebrew is *etzah*. It is "the gift of forming right conclusions" (Keil and Delitzsch, p. 183). It implies "the ability to devise an adequate plan for the situation that is being confronted, or to plot a comprehensive strategy" (Leupold, p. 217).

*Might* in Hebrew is *geburah*. It is the ability to carry out these right conclusions with energy (Keil and Delitzsch, p. 183). It is "heroic action, the ability to execute the plan" (Leupold, pp. 217 and 218).

*Knowledge of the LORD* in Hebrew is *da'ath Jehovah*. It is "knowledge founded upon the fellowship of love" (Keil and Delitzsch, p. 183). It "reaches deep. It means quite a bit more than insight into the nature and attributes of the LORD. It involves an embracing love that takes hold on the one known, refusing to let him go" (Leupold, p. 218).

*Fear of the LORD* in Hebrew is *yir'ath Jehovah*. It is "fear absorbed in reverence" (Keil and Delitzsch, p.183). It is "the deep tap root of the ruler's character: reverence for God and becoming humility" (Leupold, p. 218).

### Sheer Delight (Isaiah 11:3-4)
7/22/20

Concerning the Coronavirus pandemic, the truth is: We do not really know what the truth is. The President is now stating that it will get worse before it gets better. Hope is in the development of vaccines by competing companies, here and abroad. The ominous thought is the conspiracy theory that a vaccine will be developed that will indeed change our DNA! Hope not.

Isaiah 11:3a describes the attributes and characteristics of the Messiah: *And He will delight in the fear of the LORD ....*

Leupold writes, "In fact this last attribute is of such far-reaching importance that an explanatory clause is appended to indicate its fundamental importance, namely the word of verse 3a: *and He will delight in the fear of the LORD.* His *fear of the LORD* will not be burdensome and unpleasant but rather a matter of sheer delight. The verb used implies that this attribute constitutes the very air that the person breathes" (p. 218).

According to Keil and Delitzsch, *the fear of the LORD* is "a pleasant fragrance, for the fear of God is a pleasant sacrifice of adoration continually ascending to God" (p. 183).

I am reminded of a time when I was visiting Guatemala and was reading Psalm 1. My little granddaughter Fernanda came over to me and said in Spanish, "I can read the Bible." So I said to her, read Psalm 1. She grabbed her Spanish Bible and opened it, and to her surprise and mine also, she opened right up to Psalm 1. In Psalm 1 it says, *But his delight is in the law of the LORD and in His law he meditates day and night.*

Verse 3 concludes with the description of the Messiah:

*And He will not judge by what His eyes see,*
*Nor make a decision by what His ears hear ...*

We as humans have five senses, and here God is showing us He has senses too; but they are minimally understandable to us. Keil and Delitzsch state, "... He judges not according to outward sight, neither does he pass sentence according to outward hearing ... He does not judge according to outward appearance, but according to the relation of the heart of His God" (p. 183). According to Leupold, "He sees more than eyes – His own or those of His servants – can detect. He knows more than the informers – mercenary or official – can supply according to what they have heard" (p. 219). In layman's terms, He doesn't judge us by the clothes we wear, and He doesn't listen to gossip.

Verse 4 continues: *But with righteousness He will judge the poor, and decide with fairness for the afflicted of the earth; ... "* The word *decide* is an "official verdict" (Leupold, p. 219). "The recipients of the benefits of the Messiah's reign are the lowly and the meek. He does not overlook the unimportant people. If they get their rights, everyone else surely will" (Leupold, p 219). This is the standard according to which He will judge when saving and will judge when punishing (Keil and Delitzsch, p. 183).

When teaching a Bible study on the Gospel of John many years ago, it struck me that the lowly of society were the ones who witnessed Jesus' miracles. The following story was recorded in John, Chapter 2. At a wedding in Cana of Galilee, they were running out of wine; and Jesus' mother asked Him for help. He said to her that His time had not yet come, but she insisted. So He ordered the water pots to be filled with water. The water miraculously changed into wine:

> [9] *And when the headwaiter tasted the water which had become wine, and did not know where it came from (but*

> *the servants who had drawn the water knew), the headwaiter called the bridegroom,* ¹⁰ *and said to him, "Every man serves the good wine first, and when men have drunk freely, then that which is poorer wine; you have kept the good wine until now"* (John 2:9-10).

So the servants were the ones who were able to witness the miracle.

### Bold, Confident Leader and Judge (Isaiah 11:4-5)
7/23/20

Shall we look a little further into the characteristics of the Messiah that Isaiah described? Verse 4 of Chapter 11 continues: *And He will **strike** the earth with the rod of His mouth,* [Bold font is for emphasis]. Leupold says the word in bold is to be translated ***smite***, referring to a "befitting punishment." The recipients are the "wrong-doers, the earthly-minded, the wicked" (pp. 219-220).

Verse 4 concludes: *And with the breath of His lips He will slay the wicked.* He accomplishes this with His breath – with "effortless ease" (Leupold, p. 219). Keil and Delitzsch reference a parallel in the New Testament, citing 2 Thessalonians 2:8a: *And then that lawless one will be revealed whom the Lord will slay with the breath of His mouth* (p. 184).

Let's take a look at verse 5:

> *Also righteousness will be the belt about His loins,*
> *And faithfulness the belt about His waist.*

Flowing garments are prevented from entangling a man by use of the belt or girdle. The Lord is "never entangled in contradictions and subsequent difficulties" (Leupold, p. 220). This is a ruler who will be rock solid. His leadership will be impeccable.

### The Wolf and the Lamb in Harmony (Isaiah 11:6-7)

8/3/20

On this day, our current situation is stranger than strange. Facebook is blocking posts and claiming that they are untrue, hateful, or racist. I wouldn't mind Facebook doing this if these comments were indeed untrue, hateful, or racist; however, apparently, Facebook has deemed what is and what isn't and has become the new moral compass for our world.

Verse 6 continues with a survey of the striking results of the Messiah's reign:

> *And the wolf will dwell with the lamb,*
> *And the leopard will lie down with the kid,*
> *And the calf and the young lion and the fatling together;*
> *And a little boy will lead them.*

This depiction of the future Kingdom is very encouraging. What were considered enemies and foes in the animal world will coexist peacefully. Animals traditionally hostile to each other are now pictured as friends (Leupold, p. 221).

The passage shows that the animals are arranged by pairs, "one formerly wild, one tame" (Leupold, p. 221). "Each animal is coupled with that one which is its natural prey" (Jamison, Fausett, and Brown, p. 522).

The verse concludes with the assertion that a little child will lead these unlikely pairs of animals. It's a picture of a child of tender years leading a lot of animals out to pasture single-handedly, without trouble. All ferocity is gone (Leupold, p. 221).

I remember being way up in the beautiful mountains of Guatemala watching our niece Heidi leading a flock of sheep out to pasture. She was maybe 17, and the animals followed without a hint of doubt. They loved her and trusted her. Here we see that in the future kingdom, one much younger would be leading wolves, leopards, and lions out to pasture.

Verse 7 paints the peaceful scene with more details:

*Also the cow and the bear will graze;*
*Their young will lie down together;*
*And the lion will eat straw like the ox.*

## God's Presence and Blessing (Isaiah 11:8-9)

8/10/20

Verse 8 continues with Isaiah's astonishing description of the realities of Messiah's kingdom that will be established on earth:

*And the nursing child will play by the hole of the cobra,*
*And the weaned child will put his hand on the viper's den.*

According to Keil and Delitzsch, the snake in question is the "basilisk viper." It was supposed to have a paralyzing and bewitching influence. The Hebrew word *me'urah* is employed, which means something that exerts an attractive influence on the child, either the "blending of colors," or, better still, the "pupil of the eye ... the light of the eye ... the power of vision." However, now we see that the snake has lost its power. "It will become so tame and harmless as to let children handle its sparkling eyes as if they were jewels" (p. 185).

In Isaiah 11:9a, we see further details about the new kingdom God is promising:

*They will not hurt or destroy in all My holy mountain,*

*My holy mountain* refers to Zion, meaning Jerusalem. "The seat of the government of Messiah's throne is put for the whole earth" (Jamieson, Fausset, and Brown, p. 522). To see this, we can look back to Psalm 2, verses 6-8.

In verse 6, David writes, *"But as for Me, I have installed My King upon Zion, My holy mountain."* The Lord is speaking to David, but then a transformation occurs where the Lord is speaking to the Messiah.

Verse 7 follows, *"I will surely tell of the decree of the LORD: He said to Me, 'Thou art My Son. Today I have begotten Thee.'"*

And verse 8 continues with God's strong promise to the Messiah, *"'Ask of Me, and I will surely give the nations as Thine inheritance, and the very ends of the earth as Thy possession.'"*

Isaiah Chapter 11 verse 9b emphasizes that the whole world will recognize the Messiah, just as the sea covers the whole earth in every nook and cranny: *For the earth will be full of the knowledge of the LORD as the waters cover the sea.*

Jamieson, Fausset, and Brown state this transformation more clearly: Knowledge of the Lord will be widespread, "As the waters find their way into every cavern of its depths"; the depths of the sea (p. 522).

I was watching a movie entitled *PT-109*, a true account about JFK commanding a small vessel in the Pacific Ocean during World War II. Anticipating an imminent Japanese attack and being in a very small boat, one of the seamen said, "There sure is a lot of water out there." The reply was, "That's just the top of it."

## In that Day, On that Day (Isaiah 11:10-11)

8/12/20

By repeating the terms *in that day* and *on that day,* Isaiah announces a special day ahead for the remnant, those of his people who are found faithful.

Verse 10 puts it this way: *Then it will come about* **in that day** [Hebrew: ***bayom hahu***]. Verse 11 is the same: *Then it will happen* **on that day** [***bayom hahu***].

It's a very important day! ... *In that day ... the nations will resort to the root of Jesse.* And on that day, because the Messiah has established Himself as the secure *resting place* (verse 10) by God's enabling power, the remnant of the children of Israel will return to the Land from the four corners of the earth.

Keil and Delitzsch explain it this way: "The proud tree of the Davidic sovereignty is hewn down, and nothing is left except the root. The new David is *'shoresh Yishai,'* the root–sprout of Jesse, and therefore, in a certain sense, the root itself" (p. 186). Remember, the mention of Jesse reveals that the line of David had grown to great insignificance.

Isaiah asserts, back in Chapter 6, that Israel will not return until they are humbled enough to turn again to the Lord. Isaiah is asking how long he needs to speak to his people who are blinded to the truth. The words of reply in Isaiah 6:11-13 are striking:

> [11] *Then I said, "Lord, how long?" And He answered,*
> *"Until cities are devastated and without inhabitant,*

*Houses are without people,*
*And the land is utterly desolate,*

[12] *"The LORD has removed men far away,*
*And the forsaken places are many in the midst of the land.*

[13] *"Yet there will be a tenth portion in it,*
*And it will again be subject to burning,*
*Like a terebinth or an oak*
*Whose stump remains when it is felled.*
*The holy seed is its stump."*

If we move forward again to Isaiah, Chapter 11, verses 10 and 11, the good news is that the day of return for Israel is coming. *In that day,* Israel will return from where they are scattered.

### Again, in that Day (Isaiah 11:11-12)

8/13/20

I just received a Facebook Post from a close family member. We had been having "polite" political discussions because the elections are near. His post was very reassuring and I would post it here, but it would take too much space. Basically he encouraged us to abandon political parties and look for candidates who would help people the most. I totally agree and thanked him for his sincerity and candor.

Back to the study, verse 11 continues the description: *Then it will happen* **on that day** *[bayom hahu] that the Lord will again recover the second time with His hand the remnant of His people, who will remain,* *from Assyria, Egypt, Pathros, Cush, Elam, Shinar, Hamath, and from the islands of the sea.*

So, let's break it down. The following definitions were taken from Keil and Delitzsch (p. 187), except for one reference from Leupold when defining Pathros.

> Assyria – We know where Assyria was.
> Egypt – We know where Egypt was.
> Pathros – upper area of southern Egypt (Leupold, p. 223)
> Cush – Ethiopia, the land which lies south of Upper Egypt on both sides of the Arabian Gulf
> Elam – or Elymais, southern Media, east of the Tigris River
> Shinar – the plain to the south of the junction of the Euphrates and Tigris Rivers
> Hamath – the northern foot of Lebanon
> The islands of the sea – the islands and coastland of the Mediterranean Sea, together with the whole insular continent of Europe

Verse 12 continues: *And He will lift up a standard for the nations, and will assemble the banished ones of Israel, and will gather the dispersed of Judah from the four corners of the earth.*

### A Fraternally United Nation (11:13)

The Democratic National Convention started today, August 17, 2020. Can't wait for the debates to begin where the candidates won't have prewritten sound bites to depend on. They will have to answer real questions in real time. Back to our text.

The regathered nation of Israel that Chapter 11 describes will have a new look. Verse 13 is significant because Israel and Judah will lose their enmity toward one another; and Israel will lose its jealousy. Keil and Delitzsch note that they will become "one fraternally united nation" (p. 188).

Israel comprised the ten northern tribes, also known as Ephraim. Judah comprised the two southern tribes. They were united under David and Solomon's reign, but after Solomon died, his son Rehoboam rejected sound advice from his elder advisers and took advice from his youthful friends instead. The result was a tragic split between the two, Ephraim and Judah, that will not be reconciled until the establishment of the Messianic Kingdom.

Israel today, in a sense, is a "fraternally united nation." Jewish people from all over the world are moving to Israel for a number of reasons. Some came because of persecution during the Crusades, pogroms in Eastern Europe, and the aftermath of the Holocaust. Some come for a better life. Some come to fulfill the Messianic dream. When I went, I was hoping to discover the blessing of living in Israel.

I was in Israel two times. The first time was very romantic. I was on a tour, and we went to all the biblical, historical, and archeological sites. Praise music emanated from the PA system of the tour bus. Everything was beautiful. However, I began to realize that there were other tour busses and other tours visiting the same places. I then realized that the "real" Israel must be different than what we were witnessing. So, my Messianic dream of coming to the land of milk and honey was diminished a bit.

The second time to Israel, I went on my own. I stayed in youth hostels in Tel Aviv, Eilat, and Jerusalem. I got to know some of the local believers in *Yeshua* and attended their congregations. Everything was strikingly "real." I saw that Israel, in a way, was symbolically another state of the United States. They had the same problems, the same music, as well as the same political affiliations and economic woes. There was always the tension of war. The cost for goods and services was basically the same as the U.S., but the pay or salary for similar work was one-third of what you would get in the U.S.

What I learned while there was that if you are planning to live in Israel, you need to realize that it is difficult to live there, especially if you come from an affluent country. Also, if you are coming, do not expect Israel to take care of you. Do not be another burden for Israel to carry, but instead bring a talent, skill, or profession that will benefit and help build the country.

Living in Israel is to be compared to living on a land island. You really can't go east, north, or south because of hostile neighbors. And you can't go west because of the Mediterranean Sea. So, the spiritual and emotional pressure is very high.

So, I would say that the current return to Israel is not a fulfillment of what is predicted in Isaiah 11. It is certainly not the land of bliss and harmony. It might be the beginning of a movement, though. I do know that the ultra-Orthodox Jewish community in Israel is not looking at the current Land as a fulfillment of Bible prophesy because, from their perspective, the Messiah has not come yet, granted that their concept of Messiah is quite different than the one predicted in the Bible.

### *A New and Powerful Deliverance for Israel (Isaiah 11:14-16)*
8/18/20

So, let's finish Chapter 11, verses 14, 15, and 16.

> ¹⁴ *They will swoop down on the slopes of the Philistines on the west;*
> *Together they will plunder the sons of the east;*
> *They will possess Edom and Moab;*
> *And the sons of Ammon will be subject to them.*

In verse 14 we see this new union of Israel and Judah, this united country, depicted as an eagle, swooping down upon the Philistines. The same *will possess Edom and Moab, and the sons of Ammon will be subject to them.* These traditional enemies of the children of Israel will now be subject to Israel. Edom, Moab, and Ammon (to the east) are essentially what is now Jordan. The Philistines lived on the coastal plain of the Mediterranean. Today, their territory would be in the vicinity of Tel Aviv south to the end of Gaza.

> ¹⁵ *And the LORD will utterly destroy the tongue of the Sea of Egypt;*
> *And He will wave His hand over the River with His scorching wind;*
> *And He will strike it into seven streams, and make men walk over dry-shod.*

Verse 15 gives the picture of a new dynamic intervention, a new deliverance likened to the Lord's influence upon Egypt. The tongue of the Egyptian sea mentioned here is not the Nile River but one of the forks of the Red Sea (Jamieson, Fausset, and Brown, p. 523).

Just as He did for Moses in the Exodus from Egypt, He will bring about a new exodus from the north, from Assyria. Of course, Assyria is modern-day Iran, and it's fascinating to note that many Iranians prefer to call themselves Assyrians.

*He will wave His hand over the River with a scorching wind; and He will strike it into seven streams.* The river mentioned here is the Euphrates (Jamieson, Fausset, and Brown, p. 523). Such will make it easy for men to travel, so easy that He will *make men walk over dry-shod.*

And verse 16 concludes:

> *And there will be a highway from Assyria*
> *For the remnant of the people who will be left,*
> *Just as there was for Israel*
> *In the day that they came up out of the land of Egypt.*

It's comforting to know that in the future Kingdom Jewish people will be able to travel all the way from Assyria (Iran), through Syria, through Israel, and on to Egypt and back without even a hint of trouble.

We will start the last chapter of our study, Chapter 12, next time.

# Isaiah Chapter 12 What to Say on that Day

8/25/20

"I have just read Chapter 12." ___ yes

### A Psalm and a Song (Isaiah 12:1)

The Republican National Convention started yesterday. Can't wait for the debates.

So, let's begin Chapter 12. It is indeed a psalm and a song. Isaiah 12 is similar to Exodus 15. They are both songs of deliverance. In the Exodus passage, the deliverance is from Egypt, while the Isaiah passage celebrates deliverance from Assyria at that time as well as in the future, from the "great tribulation," "the time of Jacob's trouble or distress." (Jeremiah 30:7 references a Time of Jacob's Distress. This great trial is also referenced in Daniel 12:1-3 as the Time of Distress.)

According to verse 1:

> *Then you will say on that day,*
> > *"I will give thanks to Thee, O LORD;*
> > *For although Thou wast angry with me*
> > *Thine anger is turned away,*
> > *And Thou dost comfort me."*

Chapter 12 begins with another ***on that day* [*bayom hahu*]** with a repeat in verse 4, ***and in that day* [*bayom hahu*]**. The scenario is this: In the midst of the intense turmoil of the Tribulation period, the Messiah will come. He will descend from heaven with great glory and with powerful angels. Israel as a people – the remnant, the ones who have survived the Tribulation – will look up and see the One whom they have rejected for so long and, in utter astonishment, will confess Him as Messiah and Lord.

Look what it says in Zechariah 12, verse 10: *"And I will pour out on the house of David and on the inhabitants of Jerusalem, the Spirit of grace and of supplication, so that they will look on Me whom they have pierced; and they will mourn for Him as one mourns for an only son, and they will weep bitterly over Him, like the bitter weeping over a first-born."*

Also, if you will, consider Isaiah 53, verse 1, where it says, *Who would have believed our report? And to whom is the arm of the lord revealed?* (Alexander Harkavy Version). Countless Jewish people of all walks of life have found themselves in a quandary when realizing that *Yeshua*, Jesus, is the Jewish Messiah. Not him!? How could it be!? It comes after an honest search of the Scriptures. It comes after life's interventions that cannot be explained any other way.

### On that Day, You Will Say (Isaiah 12:1)

9/01/20

Now, there is a possibility that there will not be any debates for the candidates! So let's continue in Chapter 12, looking again at verse 1:

> *Then you will say on that day,*
>> *"I will give thanks to Thee, O LORD;*
>> *For although Thou wast angry with me,*
>> *Thine anger is turned away,*
>> *And Thou dost comfort me."*

You can see in these words that Israel is thankful that the Lord's anger is turned away, and they are receiving His comfort. The Hebrew verb for *turn away* has the same root as the verb for *repent*. It is the verb *shub*. It means "to turn."

In Isaiah 12:1, the Lord is "turning away" His anger. But let's not make the mistake of saying that the Lord's anger is something bad that He needs to repent of. It is His righteous anger that He is graciously "turning away."

God hates sin. He hates what it does to us. He hates the pride, the greed, the selfishness, and the self-centeredness. He hates that we think we are the masters of our own souls. He hates that we think we are little gods, so to speak. God is holy; and we, being sinful, cannot stand in His awesome presence. Being just, God has to sentence those who break the law, meaning all of us. At the same time, God is love. He wants the best for us and wants to spend eternity in fellowship with us.

So, God's holiness and love meet at the Roman execution block. It happened on the tree. (We Jewish people do not like to say *cross* because it reminds us of all the cruel persecution placed on us by Christians over the years.)

On the tree (cross), the Messiah, being God who had come in the flesh, took the full punishment of our sin on Himself. He says we have a choice. We can either take the punishment for our sin when we die, which would be an eternity separate from God in a place called Hell, or we can personally accept His substitutionary death on our behalf, and enter heaven when we die knowing that the price for our sins has already been paid.

Knowing that *Yeshua* rose from death gives us the assurance that we, too, will rise with Him to eternal life when we die, because we have put our trust in Him.

As we return to the Lord, He returns to us. Psalm 90:13-15 sensitively explains this concept:

> [13] *Do **return**, O LORD (shuvah Adonai); how long will it be? And be sorry for Thy servants.* [Emphasis is the author's.]

> [14] *"O satisfy us in the morning with Thy lovingkindness, That we may sing for joy and be glad all our days.*

> [15] *"Make us glad according to the days Thou hast afflicted us, And the years we have seen evil."*

### God Is My Yeshua (Isaiah 12:2-6)
9/11/20

Continuing in Chapter 12, let's look at verse 2:

> [2] *"Behold, God is my **salvation**; I will trust and not be afraid; For the LORD GOD is my strength and song, And He has become my **salvation**."*

As mentioned, Chapter 12 is a psalm or a song. Verse 2a, below, mirrors Exodus Chapter 15:

²ᵃ *"The LORD is my strength and song,*
*And He has become my **salvation**."*

As mentioned earlier, Exodus 15 commemorates the first exodus from Egypt. Isaiah 12 commemorates the exodus from Assyria, and, in the future, from the suffering of the Great Tribulation.

The word ***salvation*** is used twice in Isaiah 12, in verse 2 and again in verse 3. The word *Yeshua* means "deliverance, salvation." [The bold emphasis in Isaiah 12, verses 2 and 3, is mine.]

³ *Therefore you will joyously draw water*
*From the springs of **salvation**.*

One can't help but recount the exchange between *Yeshua* and the "woman at the well." Jesus, *Yeshua*, had to pass through Samaria, heading north to the Galilee. Usually one would avoid Samaria because it was inhabited by mixed bloods. It was the custom for conquering nations to move the people conquered over to another part of the world, and to replace them with conquered people from other parts of the world. That's what happened in Samaria. In time there was intermarriage between the indigenous Jewish population and those from other parts of the world. Such were the Samaritans.

It was dangerous to travel in Samaria; so, in order to avoid that area, most people would head east, cross the Jordan River, head north, and then head back west to where they wanted to go. On His journey,

*Yeshua* did not take the safe route but went straight north through Samaria. There he met a woman who was drawing water at Jacob's well. Being thirsty, *Yeshua* asked her for a drink. As the conversation continued, He told the woman that He had water such that, if she would drink it, she would never thirst again. Intrigued, she inquired where she could get this water, and the conversation ensued. (See the Gospel of John, Chapter 4, for all the details. You can easily find the Gospels online to review for free at websites such *as www.biblegateway.com*.)

Of course, *Yeshua* was talking to the woman at the well about the water *from the springs of salvation.* Because Yeshua's name literally meant "salvation," it was the water from the springs of *Yeshua. Yeshua's* words to the woman were: *"... Whoever drinks of the water that I shall give him shall never thirst; but the water that I shall give him shall become in him a well of water springing up to eternal life"* (John 4:14).

### What Will You Say in that Day? (Isaiah 12:4-6)

Looking back at Isaiah, Chapter 12, we see that verses 4 through 6 emphasize our joy in response to God:

> [4] *And in that day you will say,*
> *"Give thanks to the LORD, call on His name.*
> *Make known His deeds among the peoples;*
> *Make them remember that His name is exalted."*
>
> [5] *Praise the LORD in song, for He has done excellent things;*
> *Let this be known throughout the earth.*
>
> [6] *Cry aloud and shout for joy, O inhabitant of Zion,*
> *For great in your midst is the Holy One of Israel.*

### This Is One's True Expression of Faith

These final verses (Isaiah 12, verses 4 through 6), exemplify one's sincere expression of faith. It must be from the heart. It can't be burdensome. It can't be a work ethic. You can't say, "I am doing a good thing by going door to door telling people about the Lord." It won't get you favor when considering salvation. Works never work. If you have a love for the Lord and appreciate very much how He has rescued you from the despair of this world, then you have something to talk about. If you recognize how much He has sacrificed on your behalf, then you can't but tell others of the great works He has done.

Accepting the Lord has many forms. There are not many roads or paths to God as in various religions. There is only one way, not many; one path to faith in Messiah, not many. Some accept Messiah *Yeshua* by praying a scripted prayer. Others accept Him by an action such as standing up or kneeling or coming forward. Others accept Him by simply expressing their need in their innermost being.

Nonetheless, everyone who comes to Him is acknowledging in their hearts that there is a deep need for healing. There is a spiritual void that needs to be filled.

Theologically, we can say that we are incapable of entering heaven in our own strength. In order to get to heaven one needs to be perfect, and none of us is perfect. Not only that, but we all have a nature that drifts toward selfishness, pride, and arrogance. In other words, we all, by our nature, sin. We think we are good, but inside we have a condition that lurks and hides behind our goodness. We may not be aware of it, but it is there. For example, we have to teach our kids over and over again to be caring, loving, and sharing. Yet we don't have to teach them to be disrespectful, disobedient, and selfish. That comes naturally.

God is love, and God loves us deeply, but He cannot coexist with our nature of sin because He is holy and heaven is a holy place. We learn from the Scriptures that our sin nature is subject to God's righteous judgment. As we saw in the study of Isaiah, Israel's sins led to God's judgment. In the same way, our sin is also subject to judgment; and there is a place called Hell for that. So this creates a dilemma. God loves us and wants us to be with Him forever, but He is also righteous and has to judge our shortcomings, our sin nature. Still, without His provision, our punishment would be an eternity separate from Him, an eternity without love, joy, peace, and comfort. Separation from God would be a lonely and isolated existence without friends, family, or communication, a place of torment.

So, God came to earth on a rescue mission. He rescued us from the torment and punishment of sin by taking this full punishment upon Himself! He died and rose from death. He demonstrated that He had the power to grant us a pardon and bestow eternal life. It's a gift and a passage, a powerful deliverance, a way out, an exchange. We can accept this gift by thanking Him for taking our place in judgment and asking Him to come inside our heart and life, and to cleanse us from the effects of our shortcomings, our sin. He will joyfully do so because He has paid in full the judgment for our sin. By His rising from death, He shows us that we too have risen from death spiritually and will, when we die, have a joyous eternal life with Him in heaven.

Realize though that when you do accept Messiah *Yeshua* into your heart and life, your life will change for the better. Your thoughts will change. Your world view will gain a new perspective. All this will happen because you will gain a new, abiding, personal relationship with Almighty God! Old things will pass away; all things will become new.

So, accepting Jesus, *Yeshua,* has many forms. It can be a silent heart-felt prayer or an announcement to a large group, "I believe." It can be by praying a prescribed prayer written in a booklet or by walking up to the front of a sanctuary to acknowledge faith. It can be by immersion. It can be by simply waking up one morning and realizing that you suddenly believe. Nonetheless, whatever the method, the important thing is the special encounter with Almighty God, expressing deep need for forgiveness and healing, and an acceptance of His life and love in our hearts.

# Isaiah Final Thoughts

Harold Mozell 9/30/20

The renowned scholar Dr. Charles Lee Feinberg wrote this at the beginning of his commentary on Zechariah: "One who has never attempted a commentary on a book of the Bible cannot know the feeling of inadequacy that overwhelms a writer who has completed such a task. But the benefits of such an experience are incalculable. To fellowship with the heart and mind of the writer who was wrought upon of the Spirit of God is an unforgettable experience of lasting value" (Feinberg, preface p. vii).

Having known Dr. Feinberg during my time at Talbot Seminary, I found him to be genuine and human and, of course, a profound scholar. My experience at Talbot, being under the tutelage of men like Dr. Feinberg, gave me a respect for the written Word which I have carried with me through all these years.

It is my hope that those who have read this study will put two and two together and realize that *Yeshua*, Jesus, is indeed the prophesied Jewish Messiah and that they will be able to express their need for Him. Also, for those who already know the Lord, that it will give them a sense of studying the Scripture from a Jewish perspective.

As Larry Feldman, congregational leader of Shuvah Yisrael Messianic Congregation once said, when completing a study of Deuteronomy, "I feel like I'm leaving an old friend." I feel the same way and will miss Isaiah, but I am encouraged that the Lord has shown me that I have many more studies to complete before my time on this earth is over and I enter into His bliss.

# Update on Current Events

8/15/23

I called this section "Update on Current Events" because if I put these thoughts in the appendix somewhere, you might not read it. I wanted to record that much has happened since the last post.

The Coronavirus outbreak is now seemingly in check, but we are still wary of what might happen next.

The 2020 election is over. In retrospect, I believe the then-standing President lost the election because of his conduct in his first debate. After the results of the election were tallied, and a winner was declared; the claim was that the election was rigged. On the day the election results were to be certified, January 6$^{th}$, a mob actually forced their way into the Capitol building, and the unwelcome visitors were intent on killing the Vice President and the Speaker of the House!

Today, the Senate took a vote to impeach the former President for inciting a coup. Actually, the impeachment process was to prevent him from ever being able to run again. Because there was needed a two-thirds majority vote, the Senate ultimately voted to acquit the former President! Since then, there have been many attempts to discredit the former president; but after each attempt, his popularity grows more.

Since my last post, Russia has invaded Ukraine. In our attempt to help Ukraine, we are finding ourselves in a difficult political quagmire.

So, let's take the attitude of my Uncle Bert. He amazed me when I was, say, in my junior high years. He said that he does not only read the

*New York Times,* because he wanted to find out the whole truth. Being Jewish from a liberal Jewish home, that was akin to blasphemy! He wanted to read different news sources from different points of view and felt the truth was somewhere in the middle.

Likewise, it is my conviction that neither the Democrats nor the Republicans are telling the whole truth, and that the truth is somewhere in the middle of both camps.

We pray for our country to persevere and make good choices for the future, for us and for our kids and generations to come.

# Appendix

Chapter 11 of Isaiah begins with the image of a small shoot springing up from the trunk or roots of a cut down tree. It is not one of the trees from the forest mentioned in Chapter 10 that referred to the massive, strong army of Assyria. It is a different tree, one that has been humbled and laid low. It is a symbol of the Messianic line of David which has grown to such insignificance that it has been reduced to a tree stump.

Verse 1 of Chapter 11 has Hebrew words that vary in meaning from translation to translation that describe this shoot:

*Then a **choter** will spring from the **geza** of Jesse, and a **netzer** from his roots will bear fruit.*

The Hebrew word *choter* has been translated "TWIG," "SHOOT," or "ROD."

The Hebrew word *geza* has been translated "STEM," "STUMP," or "STOCK."

The Hebrew word *netzer* has been translated "BRANCH" or "SHOOT."

To see how different Bible versions translate *choter, geza, and netzer*, I have created a comparison for you to examine the subtleties in the opening verse of Isaiah Chapter 11:

*A **choter** will spring from the **geza** of Jesse, and a **netzer** from his roots will bear fruit*

King James Version:

*a **rod** out of the **stem** of Jesse, and a **BRANCH** shall grow out of his roots*

New American Standard Bible 1977:

*a **<u>shoot</u>** will spring from the **stem** of Jesse, and a **BRANCH** from his roots will bear fruit*

American Standard Version:

*a **<u>shoot</u>** out of the **stock** of Jesse, and a **BRANCH** out of his roots shall bear fruit*

Darby Translation:

*a **<u>shoot</u>** out of the **stock** of Jesse, and a **BRANCH** out of his roots shall be fruitful*

New English Translation:

*A **<u>shoot</u>** will grow out of Jesse's **root stock**; a **bud** will sprout from his roots*

English Standard Version:

*a **<u>shoot</u>** from the **stump** of Jesse, and a **BRANCH** from his roots shall bear fruit*

New International Version:

*A **shoot** will come up from the **stump** of Jesse; from his roots a **BRANCH** will bear fruit*

Look at how our commentators that I mainly used for this study translate the same verse:

Ironside (p. 75):
*And there shall come forth a **rod** out of the **stem** of Jesse, and a **BRANCH** shall grow out of its roots.*

Leupold (p. 215):
*And there shall go forth a **shoot** out of the **stump** of Jesse, and a **sprout** from its roots shall bear fruit.*

Keil & Delitzsch (p. 182):
*And there cometh forth a **twig** out of the **stump** of Jesse, and a **shoot** from its roots bringeth forth fruit.*

Hengstenberg (p. 459):
*And there cometh forth a **twig** from the **stump** of Jesse, and a **BRANCH** from its roots bringeth forth fruit.*

Now we will look at how Paraphrase Versions translate this verse. (For your information, when you read a paraphrase Bible, it is as if you are reading another Bible commentary. Paraphrases do not give a word-by-word translation, but attempt to capture the gist of the verse, taking into account word studies, context, and other scholarly methods to make the text more understandable to a contemporary reader.)

The Living Bible:

*The royal line of David will be cut off, chopped down like a tree; but from the **stump** will grow a **<u>Shoot</u>** – yes a new **BRANCH** from the old root.*

Good News Translation:

*The royal line of David is like a tree that has been cut down; but just as new **branches sprout** from a **stump**, so a new king will arise from among David's descendants.*

Hebrew and English Lexicon of the Old Testament:

Brown, Driver, and Briggs, editors of the *Hebrew and English Lexicon of the Old Testament,* report that ***choter*** is **"branch," "twig," or "rod"** (p. 310); and they reference Proverbs 14:3 which reads, "In the mouth of the foolish is a *rod* for his back" (NASB).

Brown, Driver, and Briggs also report that ***geza*** is **"stock"** or **"stem"** (p. 160).

At times, it is good to consult a reliable dictionary to lend a helping hand:

*The American Heritage College Dictionary* defines **stock** as "the trunk or main stem of a tree or another plant," "the original progenitor of a family line, ancestry or lineage" (p. 1359).

Because *stock* refers to a family line, I would say that translating *geza* as "stock" makes the most sense.

**My conclusion on Isaiah 11:1 word studies:**

From what I have been able to gather, each translator expresses the meaning of these various Hebrew words according to what they believe is the degree of difficulty that a shoot would be able to appear. For example, it would be more difficult for a shoot to grow from a root or stump than from a stem.

**Bible Translations used in this Appendix, but not elsewhere in this book:**

Scripture taken from the Good News Translation in Today's English Version, Second Edition Copyright © 1992 by American Bible Society. Used by Permission.

Scripture quoted by permission. Quotations designated (NET) are from the NET Bible® copyright ©1996, 2019 by Biblical Studies Press, L.L.C. http://netbible.com All rights reserved.

# Reference List

Baron, David. 1981. *The Visions & Prophecies of Zechariah.* Grand Rapids, MI: Kregel Publications.

Bimson, J. J., and J. P. Kane. 1985. *New Bible Atlas.* Wheaten, IL: Tyndale House Publishers, Inc.

Brown, Francis, Samuel Rolles Driver, and Charles Augustus Briggs, eds. 1977 reprint (originally published in 1907). *Hebrew and English Lexicon of the Old Testament.* New York, NY: Clarendon Press.

Bunyan, John. 1681. *The Pilgrim's Progress.* Public domain.

Cooper, David L. 1933 (Last accessed on 9/6/2022). *Messiah: His Nature and Person.* Messianic Series, Volume Two. CA: Biblical Research Society, 1933, digitized by Biblical Research Studies Group, biblicalresearch.info.

Feinberg, Charles L. *God Remembers, A Study of the Book of Zechariah.* La Mirada, CA: American Board of Missions to the Jews, 1965.

Fleming, Rocky. N.d. *The Journey: The Participant Manual.* Bella Vista, AK: Prayer Cottage publications in cooperation with CSN Books, San Diego, CA.

Fruchtenbaum, Arnold G. 2021. *Bible Study on Isaiah.* San Antonio, TX: Ariel Ministries.

Fruchtenbaum, Arnold G. N.d. *The Book of Isaiah,* cassette series (18 tapes).

Cassette 1 of 18 (side one); Isaiah 1:1-9
Cassette 1 of 18 (side two) Isaiah 1:10 – 4:1
Cassette 2 of 18 (side one) Isaiah 4:2 – 6:1
Cassette 2 of 18 (side two) Isaiah 6:1 – 7:10
Cassette 3 of 18 (side one) Isaiah 7:10 – 8:1
Cassette 3 of 18 (side two) 8:1 – 9:12
Cassette 4 of 18 (side one) 9:13 – 11:2
Cassette 4 of 18 (side two) 11:2 – 14:1

Note: Camp Shoshanah Series, circa 2009 is no longer being produced as a cassette tape series; see the DVD of the same name, which contains analogous material on 7 DVDs recorded live, available from www.ariel.org/store.

Hengstenberg, E. W. N.d. *Christology of the Old Testament.* Vol. 1. Mac Dill AFB, FL: Mac Donald Publishing Company.

Ironside, H. A. 1952. *The Prophet Isaiah.* Neptune, NJ: Loizeaux Brothers.

Jamieson, Robert; A. R. Fausset, and David Brown. 1979. *Commentary Practical and Explanatory on the Whole Bible.* Grand Rapids, MI: Zondervan Publishing House.

Keil, C. F. and F. Delitzsch. 2001. *Commentary on the Old Testament.* Vol. 7, *Isaiah.* Reprinted from the English edition originally published 1866-91 by T & T Clark. Edinbergh; Peabody, MA Hendrickson Publishers, Inc.

Leupold, H. C. 1971. *Exposition of Isaiah.* Grand Rapids, MI: Baker Book House.

Lewis, C. S. 1950-1956. *Narnia.* (A series of fantasy books first published by Macmillan Press and later by HarperCollins in 1994.)

McClain, Alva J. 1974. *The Greatness of the Kingdom.* Winona Lake, IN: BMH Books.

Ryrie, Charles Caldwell. 1995 update. *Ryrie Study Bible.* Chicago, IL: Moody Publishers.

Scofield, C. I. 1967 revision of the 1917 original version. *The Scofield Study Bible III NASB.* Edited by Walvoord, John F., Alva J. McClain, Wilbur Smith, Allen A. MacRae, Charles L. Feinberg, and Clarence Mason and others. Oxford, England: Oxford University Press. (This version of the *Scofield Study Bible* was no longer in print at the time of publishing of this book.)

Smith, F. LaGard. 2008. *The Daily Bible Experience.* Eugene, Oregon: Harvest House Publishers.

ten Boom, Corrie, with John and Elizabeth Sherrill. 1974. *The Hiding Place.* New York, NY: Bantam Books.

*The American Heritage College Dictionary.* Fourth edition. 2002. Boston, MA: Houghton Mifflin.

Walvoord, John F. 1974. *Matthew Thy Kingdom Come.* Chicago, IL: Moody Press.

Young, Robert. 1975. *Analytical Concordance to the Bible*. Grand Rapids, MI: Eerdmans Publishing Company.

# Study Outline

Acknowledgements ................................................................. xi

Foreword by Mitch Glaser ..................................................... xv

Why I Wrote This Book ............................................................. 1

Isaiah Chapter 1   A Call for Sincerity ..................................... 5

   *Isaiah's Introduction to His Book of Prophecy (Isaiah 1:1)* ............... 5
   *The Courtroom (Isaiah 1:2-15)* ............................................................ 6
   *What God Desires for His People (Isaiah 1:16-18)* ........................ 8
   *Color Systems in Language (Isaiah 1:18b-31)* ............................... 11
   *God's Transforming Color Scheme* ................................................... 11

Isaiah Chapter 2   A Call for a Humble Heart ........................ 15

   *Isaiah Shares a Refreshing Second Vision, One of Hope*
      *Isaiah 2:1, 2)* ................................................................................. 15
   *Come Let Us Go Up (Isaiah 2:1-3)* ................................................... 17
   *More Encouragement, Eagerness, and Invitations*
      *(Isaiah 2:3-5)* ................................................................................. 20
   *To See or Not to See (Isaiah 2:6)* ...................................................... 21
   *Silver and Gold Have I None (Isaiah 2:7-11)* .................................. 22
   *A Day of Reckoning (Isaiah 2:12-22)* ............................................... 23

Isaiah Chapter 3   Judah's Collapse ........................................ 25

   *Losses and Role Reversals (Isaiah 3:1-8)* ....................................... 25
   *One's Heart Brings Consequences, Good or Bad*
      *(Isaiah 3:9-15)* ............................................................................... 27
   *Figurehead or True Leader? (Isaiah 3:12-15; Isaiah 4:1)* ............. 28
   *Outer or Inner Beauty (Isaiah 3:16-26)* ........................................... 29

Isaiah Chapter 4   A Sudden Transformation ......................... 31

   *The Branch Introduced (Isaiah 4:2)* ................................................. 31

*Recorded for Life and Called Holy (Isaiah 4:3-4)* ............................ 33
*Clouds by Day and Fire by Night (Isaiah 4:5-6)* ............................... 34

Isaiah Chapter 5   The Song of My Beloved Concerning His Vineyard ................................................................................... 37

*God's Vineyard, The Perfect Parable (Isaiah 5: 1-5)* ..................... 37
*Sometimes Our Hard Work Does not Produce Fruit (Isaiah 5:1-7)* ................................................................................ 39
*Oy Vay! (Isaiah 5:11-17)* ................................................................ 41
*A Bunch of Woes, Many Oy's! (Isaiah 5:18-21)* ............................. 45
*A Wildfire Is A-Coming (Isaiah 5:22-24)* ....................................... 47
*God's Hand Is Still Stretched Out (Isaiah 5:25-30)* ........................ 49

Isaiah Chapter 6   "Whom Shall I Send?" ............................................... 53

*Before and After (Isaiah 6:1-3)* ...................................................... 53
*Two's Company; Three's a Triunity (Isaiah 6:3)* ............................ 55
*Too Loud – Too Old (Isaiah 6:4-5)* ................................................. 58
*"Depart from Me for I Am a Sinful Man, Oh Lord!" (Luke 5:8) – (Isaiah 6:5-6)* ............................................................................ 60
*Hineni: Here I Am! (Isaiah 6:8-9)* .................................................. 62

Isaiah Chapter 7   "Ask for a Sign" ......................................................... 67

*The Freedom to Question (Isaiah 7:1, 14)* ....................................... 67
*A Deeper Look (Isaiah 7:1-3)* ......................................................... 69
*"The Only Thing We Have to Fear Is Fear Itself" (Isaiah 7:4-12)* ............................................................................ 71
*I Will Not Ask (Isaiah 7:10-12)* ...................................................... 73

Isaiah Chapter 8   Do Not Fear What They Fear ..................................... 77

*Immanuel, Continued (Isaiah 8:1-4)* ............................................... 77
*Expect the Unexpected (Isaiah 8:5-8, 10)* ....................................... 79
*Is It Treason to Tell the Truth? (Isaiah 8:11-15)* ............................ 80
*Some Will Understand (Isaiah 8:16-22)* ......................................... 82

Isaiah Chapter 9   "And His Name Will Be Called" ..................85
   *Out of Darkness into Light (Isaiah 9:1)*..................................85
   *Three Points of View (Isaiah 9:1-2)*.....................................88
   *The Key of Promise (Isaiah 9:1, 2)*......................................90
   *Have Seen, Will See (Isaiah 9:2)* ........................................92
   *Rejoicing and Restoration (Isaiah 9:3-5, 6)* .......................94
   *What Is His Name? (Isaiah 9:6)* ..........................................96
   *Wonderful! (Isaiah 9:6)* ........................................................98
   *More than a Counselor (Isaiah 9:6)* ..................................101
   *All Powerful for the Good (Isaiah 9:6)*..............................103
   *Father Forever (Isaiah 9:6-7)* ............................................105
   *Beth Sar Shalom (Isaiah 9:6)*.............................................107
   *Clara and Joe (Isaiah 9:6)*..................................................109
   *Hilda (Isaiah 9:6)* ...............................................................111
   *Dr. Feinberg (Isaiah 9:6)* ...................................................111
   *Dad (Isaiah 9:6)*..................................................................112
   *"That's the Peace I've Been Telling You About"*
      *(Isaiah 9:6* ................................................................... 114
   *True World Peace (Isaiah 9:7)* ...........................................115
   *They Wanted to Build Back Better (Isaiah 9:8-12)*............116
   *Turn Toward or Turn Away? (Isaiah 9:13)* .......................118
   *Unreliable in Many Ways (Isaiah 9:14-21)* .......................119

Isaiah Chapter 10   Assyria's Conquests and Assyria's Demise ...........121
   *Are We Protecting the Needy, Poor, Widows, and Orphans?*
      *(Isaiah 10:1-4)*..............................................................121
   *The Rod of My Anger (Isaiah 10:5-10)*..............................122
   *Pride and Prejudice (Isaiah 10:10-14)*...............................123
   *A Wasting Disease, A Consuming Fire (Isaiah 10:15-19)*...124
   *On What or Whom Do We Depend? (Isaiah 10:20-23)*......126
   *There Will Always Be a Remnant (Isaiah 10:21-23)* ........127
   *A New Perspective (Isaiah 10:24)* .....................................128
   *Do Not Fear (Isaiah 10:24-26)* ..........................................130
   *Tremendous Hope (Isaiah 10:27)* .......................................132
   *Assyria's March Abruptly Shut Down (Isaiah 10:28-32)* ...135
   *A Child Can Write Them Down (Isaiah 10:19-34)* ............136

Isaiah Chapter 11   Tremendous Hope for the Future........................... 141
- *A Humble Beginning (Isaiah 11:1)* ............................................... 141
- *Degrees of Difficulty* ..................................................................... 142
- *A Persistent Life (Isaiah 11:2)* ....................................................... 146
- *The Seven-Branched Menorah (Isaiah 11:2)* ................................. 148
- *Sheer Delight (Isaiah 11:3-4)* ........................................................ 150
- *Bold, Confident Leader and Judge (Isaiah 11:4-5)* ....................... 153
- *The Wolf and the Lamb in Harmony (Isaiah 11:6-7)* ..................... 154
- *God's Presence and Blessing (Isaiah 11:8-9)* ................................ 155
- *In that Day, On that Day (Isaiah 11:10-11)* .................................. 157
- *Again, in that Day (Isaiah 11:11-12)* ............................................ 158
- *A Fraternally United Nation (11:13)* ............................................ 159
- *A New and Powerful Deliverance for Israel (Isaiah 11:14-16)* ..... 162

Isaiah Chapter 12   What to Say on that Day ........................................ 165
- *A Psalm and a Song (Isaiah 12:1)* ................................................. 165
- *On that Day, You Will Say (Isaiah 12:1)* ...................................... 166
- *God Is My Yeshua (Isaiah 12:2-6)* ................................................ 168
- *What Will You Say in that Day? (Isaiah 12:4-6)* .......................... 170
- *This Is One's True Expression of Faith* ........................................ 171

Isaiah Final Thoughts ........................................................................ 175

Update on Current Events................................................................. 177

Appendix ........................................................................................... 179

Reference List................................................................................... 185

Study Outline .................................................................................... 189

About the Author .............................................................................. 193

## About the Author

Harold Mozell is a retired instructor of English as a Second Language (ESL) which he taught in Southern California at Coastline Community College and the Huntington Beach Adult School.

Harold holds a New Jersey multi-subject teaching credential from Fairleigh Dickinson University, Madison, NJ, and a California CLAD multi-subject teaching credential from California State University Dominguez Hills, Carson, CA. He earned a Masters in English with an emphasis in teaching English as a Second Language from the same school.

Harold also attended Talbot Theological Seminary in La Mirada, CA, where he studied Bible, Theology, and Biblical languages.

A beloved evangelist, encourager, and musician, Harold has served with Chosen People Ministries and also Jews For Jesus. He has taught children and adults the Bible for 50 years.

Being from a musical family, he has learned to play tenor banjo, five-string banjo, mandolin, and guitar. He is presently attending Shuvah Yisrael Messianic Congregation in Irvine, CA, where he is part of the worship team and teaches in the Shabbat School.

www.ingramcontent.com/pod-product-compliance
Lightning Source LLC
Chambersburg PA
CBHW071417160426
43195CB00013B/1724